P9-AQG-322

ANDREW JOHNSON
1808 - 1875

Chronology - Documents - Bibliographical Aids

Edited by
John N. Dickinson

Series Editor
Howard F. Bremer

1970
OCEANA PUBLICATIONS, INC.
Dobbs Ferry, New York

Library of Congress Catalog Card Number: 79-116064
International Standard Book Number: 0-379-12075-5

Manufactured in the United States of America

CONTENTS

EDITOR'S FOREWORD

Every attempt has been made to cite accurate dates in this Chronology. Diaries, documents, and similar sources have been used to determine the exact date. Sometimes even original source materials give conflicting dates. In these cases, with the help of later scholarship, the more plausable date has been listed. Should this Chronology be in conflict with other authorities, the student is urged to consult original sources.

This is a research tool compiled primarily for the student. While it does make some judgments on the significance of events, it is hoped that they are reasoned judgments based on a long acquaintance with American History. Obviously, the very selection of events by any writer is itself a judgment.

The essence of these little books is in their making available some pertinent facts and key documents plus a critical bibliography which should direct the student to investigate additional material. The works cited may not always be available in small libraries, but neither are they usually the old, out of print type of books often included in similar accounts. Documents in this volume are taken from James D. Richardson, ed., Messages and Papers of the Presidents Vols. V and VI; Washington, 1910.

CHRONOLOGY

CHRONOLOGY

YOUTH AND EARLY POLITICS

1808

December 29   Born, Raleigh, North Carolina. Father: Jacob Johnson. Mother: Mary McDonough Johnson. Named Andrew Johnson.

1812

January 4   Death of Jacob Johnson.

1822

February 18   Apprenticed to James J. Shelby, a tailor of Raleigh.

1824

June 15   Ran away from his master.

Summer   Opened tailor shop in Carthage, North Carolina.

Winter   Moved to Laurens, South Carolina.

1825

Spring   Returned to Raleigh possibly to try to reach a settlement with his former master.

1826

Summer   Left Raleigh with his mother and stepfather Turner Daugherty to move west.

September   Arrived at Greeneville, Tennessee.

1827

March   Opened tailor shop in Greeneville.

May 17   Married Eliza McCardle who assumed the responsibility for his education.

1

1828

Spring   Organized a "Workingman's Party" in Greeneville.

October 25   Birth of daughter Martha.

1829

Spring   Elected Alderman of Greeneville and subsequently re-elected twice.

1830

February 19   Birth of son Charles.

1832

May 8   Birth of daughter Mary.

Spring   Elected Mayor of Greeneville and subsequently re-elected twice.

1834

February 22   Birth of son Robert.

1835

Fall   Elected to the lower house of the Tennessee Legislature from Greene and Washington Counties.

1836

Summer   Supported Whig candidate Hugh Lawson White of Tennessee for President against Martin Van Buren.

1837

Fall   Badly defeated for re-election after opposing a road system needed by his two counties.

1839

Fall   Elected to the lower house again.

1840

Fall   Candidate for Presidential Elector for Tennessee but defeated in the Harrison landslide.

1841

Fall   Elected to the Tennessee State Senate from Greene and
                     Hawkins Counties.

1843

Fall   Elected to Congress from the First District of Tennes-
                     see and served in the House for the next ten years.

1845

January 21   Told the House that he favored the admission of Texas
                     as the means whereby slaves would eventually find a
                     way to freedom.

Fall   In winning re-election to Congress defeated W. G. "Par-
                     son" Brownlow, destined to be a great political enemy.

1846

March 27   Introduced a Homestead Bill in the House. This bill
                     would grant to any family head 160 acres of public land
                     on condition of cultivation for five years. The bill was
                     passed in the House, defeated in the Senate.

1848

December 11   Announced that he intended to re-introduce the Home-
                     stead Bill and did so at every House session as long as
                     he was a member.

1850

June 5   Favored the admission of California with slavery to
                     open more opportunities for homeless whites.

July 25   Made his first major House speech in favor of the Home-
                     stead Bill.

September 12   Voted for the strict Fugitive Slave Law.

September 17   Voted against abolishing the slave trade in the District
                     of Columbia.

1852

May 27   Addressed a mass meeting in New York City on the subject of the Homestead Bill.

August 5   Birth of son Andrew

1853

April 14   Nominated by the Tennessee Democrats for Governor.

August   Elected Governor of Tennessee.

December 19   In his first message to the Tennessee Legislature he demanded more support for public schools.

1855

August   Re-elected Governor of Tennessee.

1857

October 8   Elected United States Senator by the unanimous vote of the Democratic majority in the Legislature.

1860

June 5   Declared in the Senate that Congress had no power to legislate on slavery.

June 19   His Homestead Bill passed by Congress only to receive a veto from President James Buchanan.

June   Received the votes of the twelve Tennessee delegates for Presidential nomination on thirty-six roll calls at the Democratic National Convention.

Summer   Supported John C. Breckinridge for President.

November 6   Abraham Lincoln elected Sixteenth President.

December 13   Johnson proposed a Constitutional Amendment designed to prevent the monopoly of the Federal Executive and Judiciary by any one section of the nation.

December 18   In the Senate declared for the Union, the only Southern
                 Senator to do so.

December 20   South Carolina seceded from the Union.

1861

February 5   Again defended the Union in the Senate.

March 2   In the Senate called the secession leaders "traitors."

May   Campaigned through Eastern Tennessee in behalf of the
                 Union.

May 7   The Legislature of Tennessee ratified a "Military
                 League" with the seceeding states.

June 8   In spite of his efforts Tennessee voted for secession
                 104,913 to 47,328.

July 24   Introduced a resolution on the purpose of the war.

July 27   Defended the Lincoln Administration after the First
                 Battle of Bull Run.

December 19   Made a member of the Congressional Joint Committee
                 on the Conduct of the War.

MILITARY GOVERNOR

1862

January 6   Lincoln urged General Don Carlos Buell to push into
                 Eastern Tennessee saying that Senator Johnson might
                 resign to go home to protect his family "or die with
                 them."

January 31   In the Senate described the terrible price being paid
                 by loyalists in Tennessee in areas overrun by Confed-
                 erates.

February 25   Union Army under Buell took possession of Nashville.

March 4   Appointed Military Governor of Tennessee with the rank of Brigadier General by Lincoln.

March 10   From Cincinnati requested that General Buell prepare any suggestions that might be useful.

March 11   Warned by General Buell not to expect an enthusiastic welcome to Nashville and suggested entering the city with no display.

March 12   Arrived in Nashville to assume new duties.

March 18   Issued his "Appeal to the People of Tennessee" and announced that the American flag once again flew over the state capitol.

March 22   Secretary of War Edwin M. Stanton ordered General Henry W. Halleck to provide Johnson with adequate military support.

March 25   Dismissed the pro-Confederate city government and replaced it with Union men.

March 29   Warned the War Department that General Buell had left Nashville almost defenseless. There were no artillery and only a few infantry regiments available.
                 Ordered the arrest of an ex-Mayor of Nashville.

March 30   Stanton warned Halleck of the serious consequences if Nashville should fall and directed that aid be sent to Johnson.

April 8   Confederate President Jefferson Davis imposed martial law on Eastern Tennessee.

April 23   Reported to Stanton that the 69th Ohio Regiment (infantry) had arrived for the defense of Nashville, that two home

guard regiments were complete, and four others nearly
so.

April 24   Eliza Johnson ordered by the Confederate command to
            leave Eastern Tennessee within thirty-six hours. Be-
            cause she suffered with tuberculosis, the order was re-
            scinded; but her home in Greeneville was confiscated.

April 25   Protested that the 69th Ohio that was supposed to have
            been assigned to the defense of Nashville had been taken
            away by General Buell.

April 26   Buell defended his disposition of troops and called John-
            son's view absurd.
            Carried his protest regarding the 69th Ohio directly to
            Lincoln and hinted that Buell was incompetent.

May 1   Confederate forces driven from all Tennessee except for
            the eastern section. Panic in Nashville ended.

May 11   Protested to Stanton that the failure to provide troops in
            Nashville encouraged the local secessionists and would
            limit the crowd at next day's mass meeting.

May 12   Addressed a mass meeting of Unionists in Nashville.

May 13   United States Circuit Court convened in Nashville to deal
            with "traitors."

May 14   Ordered the arrest of former Governor of Tennessee
            Neil S. Brown for treason. Later Brown was released
            on parole.

May 22   An anti-administration man elected to the state circuit
            court in the Nashville district. Johnson gave him his
            commission and then had him arrested and imprisoned.

May 24   The United States Marshal for Middle Tennessee acting
            on orders from Johnson seized the offices of the Repub-

lican Banner, Union and American, and Gazette, Nashville newspapers, and the Southern Methodist Printing House.

May 26	The office of the Baptist Publishing House in Nashville seized by United States marshals.
June 4	Issued an order providing that anyone using treasonable language would be arrested and sent to the South. If such a person returned he would be treated as a spy.
June 5	Told Lincoln that he desired the release of prisoners who were Tennessee citizens and who would be loyal to the Union in the future.
June 17	Ordered six Nashville ministers arrested for treason. Five were sent to prison and eventually sent to the South, behind Confederate lines. Complained to Halleck that the constant disputes between Union generals in Tennessee had placed the state in danger.
June 26	Urged the War Department that the Union army be subsisted on the enemy so that the Confederates would feel the full weight of the war.
July 5	Confederate capture of Lebanon, Tennessee, threatened Nashville from the east.
July 10	Complained to Lincoln that Buell's assistant adjutant-general had arrested the commander of the 69th Ohio for obeying Johnson's orders instead of Buell's.
July 11	Lincoln told Johnson to put his faith in General Halleck, and that Johnson could not expect to be placed in full command of the west.
July 12	Lincoln ordered the commanding officer of the 69th Ohio released and ordered the arresting officer out of Nashville.

July 13   Warned Halleck that the Confederates were attacking
                 Murfreesboro. In the event of an attack on Nashville,
                 Johnson promised, "as warm a reception as we know
                 how."
                 Confederate capture of Murfreesboro threatened Nash-
                 ville from the southeast.

July 21   Confederate General Nathan B. Forrest reported to be
                 within six miles of Nashville.

August   Nashville gradually cut off from contact with Washington
                 by Confederate forces.

August 10   Communications between Nashville and Louisville sev-
                 ered by the Confederates.

August 12   Halleck warned Buell that the administration in Wash-
                 ington had received complaints about Buell's lack of ac-
                 tivity and that there was a danger that he would be re-
                 placed.

August 21   Confederate forces under General Braxton Bragg began
                 to advance on Kentucky. If the advance had succeeded,
                 Nashville and Middle Tennessee would have been lost to
                 the Union.

August 22   Confederate forces captured Gallatin, Tennessee, cut-
                 ting the vital Louisville-Nashville railroad northeast of
                 Nashville.

September 14   General Bragg captured the supply depot at Munfordville,
                 Kentucky, again cutting the Louisville-Nashville rail-
                 road.

September 15 to Nashville virtually under state of siege, but Johnson re-
November 14   fused to consider the surrender of the city.

October 8   Bragg and Buell fought the "draw" battle of Perryville,
                 Kentucky, after which both armies returned to Tennes-

see, Buell going to Nashville.

October 30   Buell was relieved of command and replaced by General William S. Rosecrans.

December 8   Called for the election of Congressmen from the 9th and 10th Districts of Tennessee to be held December 29. A raid by General Forrest prevented the opening of the polls.

December 26   Following the "draw" battle of Murfreesboro, the Confederates retired from Middle Tennessee.

1863

January 8   Notified Lincoln that the Captain Todd killed in the battle of Murfreesboro was Charles S. Todd of Shelbyville, Kentucky, a relative of Mrs. Lincoln.

February   Made a speaking tour through Ohio, Pennsylvania, New York, and New Jersey in support of the Union cause.

March 26   In a private message Lincoln asked Johnson to take charge of the raising of 50,000 black troops. He told Johnson that as an eminent citizen of a slave state and as a slave owner he was specially qualified.

March 28   Authorized to raise ten infantry regiments, ten cavalry regiments, and ten artillery batteries.

April 2   Notified by the War Department that he had the authority to impose taxes and to take possession of the property of persons behind Confederate lines.

April 4   Death of son Dr. Charles Johnson in a horse accident.

April 18   Informed by Stanton that he had the authority to take charge of all the abandoned lands in Tennessee as well as all abandoned slaves.

April 22   In testimony before a military tribunal investigating Buell's conduct in 1862 stated that Buell could see no military value in holding Nashville.

May 5   Buell denied Johnson's claim that he intended to abandon Nashville in 1862.

August 16   Informed Lincoln that he had succeeded in raising two brigades of Tennessee volunteers and requested that a general be assigned to command them.

August 18   Suggested to Rosecrans that this would be a good time to start construction of a railroad to the northwest from Nashville.

August 23   Requested arms for 4,000 cavalrymen from Rosecrans. The War Department promised prompt delivery on the same day.

August 27   General Rosecrans asked Johnson to assume the responsibility for the construction of the northwestern railroad.

September 8   Had an interview in Nashville with Assistant Secretary of War Charles A. Dana. Dana reported Johnson to be optimistic, confident that the new Tennessee Legislature would abolish slavery, but saying that Rosecrans was too slow. Johnson regarded Rosecrans as "a patriot at heart and not a damn traitor like his predecessor (Buell)." Lincoln urged Johnson to forward all trained troops available to Rosecrans and to use untrained men, black or white, to guard the roads and bridges.

September 9   With Dana visited Union troops near Chattanooga.

September 11   Lincoln suggested to Johnson that it was time to re-establish regular government in Tennessee, but Johnson must make sure that loyal men were put in charge.

September 17   Replied to Lincoln's letter of September 11 that he was pleased and encouraged.

September 19   Lincoln officially authorized Johnson to use his power
                as Military Governor to set up a regular state govern-
                ment in Tennessee.

September 19   Union defeat in the Battle of Chickamauga again threat-
and 20   ened Middle Tennessee.

November 23   Union victory in the Battle of Chattanooga ended the
to 25   danger to Middle Tennessee.

                              1864

January 21   At a mass meeting in Nashville announced that Tennes-
                see had never been out of the Union. Johnson also
                called for a "tight" oath as a qualification for voting
                in Tennessee.

January 26   Issued a call for the election of county officers on March
                5 with a "tight" oath.

February 27   Lincoln informed the Tennessee Secretary of State that
                the oath prescribed in Johnson's January 26 proclama-
                tion was entirely satisfactory.

March 5   The election held this day was marked by scandal and
                irregularities and considered to be a farce.

April 5   Protested strongly at the rumor that Buell would be
                placed in command in Knoxville.

May 30   The Tennessee Union Party Convention meeting in Nash-
                ville urged the nomination of Johnson for Vice-President.

June 7   The National Union Party Convention in Baltimore nomi-
                nated the slate of Lincoln and Johnson.

June 10   In a speech in Nashville announced that Louis Napoleon's
                intervention in Mexico would come to an end once the

Civil War was over.

June 25	Officially notified of his nomination for Vice-President.

August 17 — Sent a plea for mercy for a young Confederate sentenced to death for murder. Johnson asked that the commutation order be sent to him to hold up until the last moment because "it would have a good moral effect . . . ." Lincoln complied.

August 29 — The Democratic National Convention meeting in Chicago nominated the slate of General McClellan and George H. Pendleton and called for a negotiated peace.

September 5 to 7 — The Tennessee Union Party Convention meeting in Nashville proposed an even "tighter" oath for the Presidential election. Voters would have to swear that they opposed a negotiated peace.

September 30 — Called for a Presidential election in Tennessee on November 8 under the terms of the Nashville Convention's "tighter" oath.

October 22 — Lincoln gave his approval to the election system in Tennessee.

November 8 — The ticket of Lincoln and Johnson won with the Tennessee vote only a formality. Since the Democratic National Platform called for a negotiated peace, any Tennessee man who voted for McClellan could be charged with perjury. The vote in Nashville was: Lincoln--1,317, McClellan--25.

December 15 and 16 — A Union Army under General George Thomas crushed a Confederate Army before Nashville marking the end of the last threat to the state.

1865

January 9 — The Tennessee Constitutional Convention met in Nashville.

January 12   Urged the Constitutional Convention to adopt amend-
                    ments abolishing slavery forever in Tennessee but to
                    leave the question of the right to vote to a later date.

January 13   The Convention yielded to Johnson's requests, and John-
                    son so notified Lincoln.

January 14   Lincoln asked Johnson to suggest the name of the next
                    Military Governor of Tennessee.

January 17   Told Lincoln that he would much prefer to remain in
                    Tennessee to turn the state over to its new government
                    than to be sworn in as Vice-President in Washington on
                    March 4.

January 24   Told by Lincoln that the Cabinet was unanimous that
                    Johnson must be in Washington on March 4.

February 6   Congress refused to count the electoral vote of Tennes-
                    see--an ill omen.

February 22   Tennessee ratified the State Constitutional Amendments
                    banning slavery by a near unanimous vote.

February 25   Left Nashville for Washington claiming the vote of Feb-
                    ruary 22 a great valedictory.

March 3   Congress created the Bureau of Refugees, Freedmen,
                    and Abandoned Lands (Freedmen's Bureau).
                    Stanton accepted Johnson's resignation as Brigadier Gen-
                    eral and Military Governor.

March 4   William G. ("Parson") Brownlow elected Governor of
                    Tennessee.

VICE-PRESIDENT AND PRESIDENT

March 4   Took the oath of office as Vice-President and made a
                    drunken speech to the Senate. Friends had given him

alcohol trying to help him recover from an illness.

April 2   The Confederate Army abandoned Richmond.

April 5   The new Tennessee Legislature ratified the Thirteenth
                 Amendment.

April 9   General Robert E. Lee surrendered the Army of North-
                 ern Virginia.

April 15   Became the Seventeenth President of the United States
                 upon the death of Lincoln.

April 16   Told several Congressional leaders: "Treason must be
                 made infamous and traitors must be impoverished."

April 18   Initial surrender terms for Confederate General Joseph
                 E. Johnston had so many political considerations that
                 Johnson ordered the surrender set aside.

April 26   Johnston surrendered on terms similar to the Grant-
                 Lee agreement.

May 1   Directed that the conspirators in the Lincoln assassina-
                 tion be tried by military tribunal.

May 2   Accused Jefferson Davis and other southern leaders of
                 complicity in the assassination of Lincoln and offered
                 a reward of $100,000 for the capture of Davis.

May 6   Appointed ten army officers as members of the military
                 tribunal to try the conspirators.

May 9   Recognized the legitimacy of the Francis Pierpont "gov-
                 ernment" in Virginia, declared Confederate authority
                 in the South to be null and void, and recognized the gov-
                 ernments established by Lincoln in Arkansas, Louisiana
                 and Tennessee.

May 10	Jefferson Davis captured.
May 22	Ordered the lifting of the blockade for most of the Southern ports.
May 23 and 24	Attended the grand review of the Army of the Potomac and the Army of the Tennessee in Washington.
May 25	The last major Confederate unit in the field surrendered.
May 29	Announced a policy of amnesty for the South which in general followed Lincoln's plan. Appointed William W. Holden Provisional Governor of North Carolina with orders to begin the restoration process within the state.
May 31	Told General John A. Logan that since the southern states had never legally left the Union reconstruction was unnecessary.
June 2	Ordered the Treasury Department to turn over to the Freedmen's Bureau all abandoned lands and property in the South.
June 13	Named William L. Sharkey Provisional Governor of Mississippi.
June 17	Appointed James Johnson and Andrew J. Hamilton Provisional Governors of Georgia and Texas.
June 21	Named Lewis E. Parsons Provisional Governor of Alabama.
June 24	Governor John Andrew of Massachusetts on behalf of the Board of Overseers invited Johnson to accept an honorary degree from Harvard. Johnson declined.
June 30	Named Benjamin F. Perry Provisional Governor of South Carolina.

July 5   Approved the sentences of the conspirators in Lincoln's assassination and ordered that four be executed on July 7. Johnson was not told that five members of the trial commission had recommended that he commute Mrs. Surratt's sentence to life imprisonment.

July 13   Appointed William Marvin Provisional Governor of Florida.

August 14   The Mississippi Constitutional Convention met, the first to do so under Johnson's plan for restoration.

August 20   Governor Sharkey of Mississippi notified Johnson that the convention would abolish slavery but that it would do nothing about the rights of blacks to vote or to testify in courts.

October 18   Warned Governor Holden that North Carolina must repudiate its war debt.
                  Urged Governor Perry of South Carolina to use his influence to get the legislature to ratify the Thirteenth Amendment.

November 1   Warned Governor Sharkey that the failure of the Mississippi Legislature to ratify the Thirteenth Amendment would bring an unfavorable reaction in the North.

November 17   Told Governor-elect Benjamin G. Humphreys of Mississippi that the state must guarantee the full civil rights of the freedmen.

November 26   Warned Governor Johnson of the unfortunate reaction should the Georgia Legislature fail to ratify the Thirteenth Amendment.

November 27   Warned Governor Holden that the North Carolina election results had brought about concern in the North because ex-Confederates were elected. Johnson asked that the new legislature be more careful.

December 2   Alabama ratified the Thirteenth Amendment complet-
                    ing the necessary three-fourths of the states to do so.

December 4   Ordered Governor Holden of North Carolina to turn
                    over the direction of the state to his elected successor.
                    The 39th Congress met for the first time and refused
                    to seat the Congressmen from the restored states (in-
                    cluding those from Johnson's Tennessee). It took the
                    first steps toward the creation of the Joint Committee
                    on Reconstruction, the committee that would consider
                    all measures dealing with the South. Johnson had had
                    thirty-three weeks in which to deal with restoration
                    without Congress.

December 6   Congress finally agreed to hear Johnson's annual mes-
                    sage. (Usually a Congress will hear the message be-
                    fore conducting any business other than the organiza-
                    tion of the House.)
                    Ex-Governor Holden warned Johnson that the Union men
                    of North Carolina were not coming forward to leader-
                    ship.

December 12   Upheld General Thomas's decision to suspend the order
                    of the Mississippi Legislature that would have disarmed
                    the freedmen.

December 14   Ordered Governor Sharkey to turn the affairs of Mis-
                    sissippi over to his elected successor.

December 18   Ordered Governor Parsons to turn Alabama over to
                    the new Governor.

December 19   Ordered Governor Johnson to yield Georgia to the new
                    Governor.

December 21   Governor Perry of South Carolina turned the state over
                    to his successor upon the orders of Johnson.

1866

January 18	Ordered Governor Marvin of Florida to turn state affairs over to the elected authorities.
January 31	The Legislature of Georgia elected former Confederate Vice-President Alexander Stevens the new United States Senator from Georgia. Knowing that this would seriously embarrass Johnson, Stevens apologized the next day; but the damage had been done.
February 6	Received from Congress a bill that would have extended the life of the Freedmen's Bureau indefinitely.
February 12	Secretary of State Seward all but ordered Louis Napoleon to get the French Army out of Mexico.
February 13	Warned Provisional Governor Hamilton of Texas that the rapid seating of the Texas delegation in Congress would depend upon the future proceedings of the Texas Constitutional Convention.
February 19	The Joint Committee on Reconstruction took the first steps toward the re-admission of Tennessee. Astounded friends and enemies alike with a veto of the extension of the Freedmen's Bureau.
February 20	The Joint Committee on Reconstruction abandoned consideration of the re-admission of Tennessee. The Senate failed to pass the Freedmen's Bureau Bill over the veto.
February 22	In a rash speech denounced Congressman Thaddeus Stevens, Senator Charles Sumner, and reformer Wendell Phillips as men laboring to destroy the fundamental principles of government.
February 23	The House without grounds voted to expel Daniel Voorhees of Indiana, a loyal Johnson man.

March 13   Received from Congress a Civil Rights Bill, a com-
                    promise measure acceptable to Congressional moder-
                    ates.

March 27   Vetoed the Civil Rights Bill.
                    The Senate expelled Democrat John P. Stockton of New
                    Jersey giving the Republicans a two-thirds majority in
                    the Senate.

April 2   Noted that a government that has successfully put down
                    a rebellion has only two choices. It can deal with the
                    former rebels in such a way that they voluntarily be-
                    come friends, or it can hold power by terror and dev-
                    astation. The second course was repugnant to humanity.

April 5   The French government announced that it would remove
                    its troops from Mexico over a period of nineteen months.

April 6   The Senate passed the Civil Rights Bill over Johnson's
                    veto by a margin of one vote.

April 9   The House passed the Civil Rights Bill over the veto
                    making this measure the first major bill to be enacted
                    into law over a President's veto.

April 30   Forty-seven black men killed in rioting in Memphis,
                    Tennessee, and eighty more wounded. The radicals
                    blamed Johnson's policies.

May 8   Radical Congressman Stevens referred to Johnson as
                    "the late lamented Andrew Johnson of blessed memory."

May 15   Vetoed an act granting statehood to Colorado on the
                    grounds of insufficient population. This veto was sus-
                    tained.

June 13   Congress submitted the Fourteenth Amendment to the
                    states for ratification.

June 15   Vetoed a bill that would have permitted the New York
                        and Montana Iron Mining and Manufacturing Company
                        to purchase tracts of public land not on the general
                        market at the time. Such a veto was consistent with
                        Johnson's concept of Jacksonian Democracy.

July   Three Radical members of the Cabinet resigned and
                        were replaced by Republicans friendly to Johnson.

July 16   Vetoed a new Freedmen's Bureau Bill. The bill was
                        then passed over the veto.

July 19   The Tennessee Legislature ratified the Fourteenth
                        Amendment, the only ex-Confederate state to do so at
                        this time. In his wire to the Senate giving this news
                        Governor Brownlow concluded with, "Give my regards
                        to the dead dog of the White House."

July 21   Congress re-admitted Tennessee to the Union by joint
                        resolution.

July 27   The transoceanic cable (broken early in the Civil War)
                        was replaced and direct communications with Europe
                        restored.

July 30   Race riot in New Orleans resulted in the death of near-
                        ly forty, mostly freedmen or Unionists. Many in the
                        North were convinced that this was the result of John-
                        son's lenient policies toward the South.

August 14   Received Queen Emma of the Hawaiian Islands.
                        Endorsed by a mass convention of Unionists in Phila-
                        delphia. This convention was often called the "Arm in
                        Arm" convention because of the method of entry of the
                        Massachusetts and South Carolina delegations. Actually
                        it was dominated by Democrats with several prominent
                        Copperheads in the vicinity.

August 28   Left Washington to begin the "Swing Around the Circle" in an attempt to defeat the Republican Radicals in the fall Congressional elections.

August 29   In New York City said, "Let my enemies slander me."

August 30   Announced in Albany that he had not come to make a speech and then proceeded to make one anyway. Johnson followed this curious habit all through the "Swing."

August 31   Expressed his appreciation for the reception given him by the people of Schenectady and Auburn.

September 1   Received by enthusiastic audiences in Niagara and Buffalo.

September 3   Received his first serious heckling in his speech in Cleveland.
In leaving Toledo stated that the Constitution was safe in the hands of the people.

September 4   In Detroit stated that he had once fought against traitors in the South and now he was fighting against them in the North.

September 5   Gave a short non-political speech in the memory of Stephen A. Douglas.

September 7   In Lamont, Bloomington, and Atlanta, Illinois, the audience was so hostile that the train conductor ordered the engineer to proceed while Johnson was still trying to speak.

September 8   So badly received in St. Louis that his tirade against the Radicals was at times incoherent.

September 12   Asked an audience in Cincinnati why he should be called a traitor when he had filled just about every elective office possible.

September 13	The Mayor of Pittsburgh refused to meet the Presidential train.
September 15	Returned to Washington
September, October, and November	The Congressional elections constituted a complete defeat for Johnson and a victory for the Radicals.
November 19	Ordered General Thomas not to turn over the civil authority in Mississippi to elected Governor Humphreys until the latter had received an executive pardon.
December 3	Requested in his second annual message to Congress that the restored states be recognized and their Congressmen granted their seats.

1867

January 7	The House instructed its Judiciary Committee to investigate charges against Johnson.
January 16	Congress again attempted to gain two more Radical Senators by passing a Colorado statehood bill.
January 22	Congress seized control of its own sessions by ordering the Fortieth Congress into session on March 4, 1867. Under the Constitution it would not have met until December, 1867, unless called sooner by Johnson.
January 28	Vetoed the Colorado bill on the grounds of insufficient population. This veto was sustained.
March 1	In an effort to secure two more Radical Senators, Congress passed the Nebraska Statehood Bill over Johnson's veto. Eventually both Nebraska Senators voted to convict Johnson. Proclaimed Nebraska to be a State in the Union.
March 2	The First Reconstruction Act passed over Johnson's veto. It was designed to destroy the existing restoration governments, and it created five military districts in the South.

Congress passed the Tenure of Office Act over Johnson's veto. It was thought that the act would prevent Johnson from removing Cabinet officers without Senate consent. The Army Appropriations Act was passed by Congress limiting Johnson's authority over the Army.

March 11   In compliance with the First Reconstruction Act appointed five major-generals as military commanders in the South: J. M. Schofield for Virginia, D. E. Sickles for the Carolinas, G. H. Thomas for Georgia, Florida, and Alabama, E. O. C. Ord for Mississippi and Arkansas, and P. H. Sheridan for Louisiana and Texas.

March 15   Replaced General Thomas with General John Pope.

March 23   Vetoed the Second Reconstruction Act which Congress re-passed the same day. Since the First Reconstruction Act failed to place the initiative for calling new elections in the hands of anyone, the new act placed it in the hands of the military commanders.

March 30   Treaty for the purchase of Alaska signed by Seward and Édouard de Stoeckl in Washington.

April 6   On a vote of 27 to 12 the Senate granted its consent to the treaty purchasing Alaska from Russia for $7,200,-000.

June 3   The House Judiciary Committee decided on a five to four vote that there was not sufficient evidence on which to impeach Johnson.

June 20   Issued a set of orders to the military commanders in the South ignoring the Reconstruction Acts.

July 19   Vetoed the Third Reconstruction Act which Congress re-passed on the same day. This act clarified election procedures in the South and countered Johnson's orders of June 20.

August 5   Johnson requested the resignation of Secretary of War
                    Stanton. The latter refused.

August 12   Suspended Secretary Stanton pending a report to the
                    Senate. General Grant agreed to be Secretary of War
                    ad interim.

August 17   Replaced Sheridan with Thomas as military commander
                    of Louisiana and Texas.

August 26   Replaced Sickles with General E. R. S. Canby as mili-
                    tary commander of the Carolinas. These changes ir-
                    ritated the Radicals.

August 28   The United States took possession of Midway Island.

September 3   In a proclamation ordered all civil and military author-
                    ities to obey the laws and the decisions of the courts.

September 7   Issued second amnesty proclamation reducing the num-
                    ber of exempt classes from fourteen to three.

November 20   On a five to four vote the House Judiciary Committee
                    recommended the impeachment of Johnson.

December 3   In his annual message to Congress stated that his con-
                    victions regarding restoration had not changed but were
                    strengthened by events.
                    Sent to the Senate for its consent the treaty between the
                    United States and Denmark stipulating the cession of
                    the Virgin Islands.

December 7   The House failed to pass an impeachment resolution
                    on a vote of 57-108.

December 12   Sent to the Senate the executive orders and documents
                    relating to the August 12 suspension of Stanton and gave
                    his reasons for his actions in this case.

1868

January 13	The Senate refused to concur with the removal of Stanton.
January 14	Grant returned possession of the War Department to Stanton and notified Johnson that he was no longer Secretary of War ad interim.
February 21	Removed Stanton from office and replaced him with General Lorenzo Thomas in apparent violation of the Tenure of Office Act.
February 22	The Joint Committee on Reconstruction recommended that the House impeach Johnson.
February 24	The House voted 126-47 to impeach the President.
March 2	The House adopted the first nine Articles of Impeachment.
March 3	The House adopted the last two Articles of Impeachment.
March 5 and 6	The Senate was sworn in as a court to try the President.
March 11	The Fourth Reconstruction Act became law after Johnson had given it a silent veto. The law provided that in the elections in the South a simple majority of those who had voted would decide an issue regardless of how few had voted.
March 13	Trial before the Senate began.
May 16	On a vote of nineteen to thirty-five the Senate acquitted Johnson on Article Eleven. The Senate then recessed to May 26.

May 20 and 21	The Republican National Convention meeting in Chicago nominated the slate of Grant and Schuyler Colfax. It declared that Johnson had been found guilty.
May 26	With the same vote as on May 16 the Senate acquitted Johnson on Articles Two and Three. The Senate immediately adjourned and never voted on the other Articles.
June 3	Ordered a day of official mourning at the death of former President James Buchanan.
June 20	Vetoed a bill re-admitting Arkansas into the Union on the grounds that a majority of its citizens would not vote because of the oath requirement.
June 22	Congress re-passed the Arkansas bill over the veto.
June 25	Vetoed a bill for the re-admission of the Carolinas, Louisiana, Georgia, Alabama, and Florida on the same grounds that he had vetoed the Arkansas bill. Congress passed the bill over the veto on the same day.
July 4	Granted full pardon to all former Confederates except for those under indictment for treason (Davis) or felony (a few others).
July 8	The Democratic National Convention meeting in New York nominated Horatio Seymour for President and Johnson's friend Francis P. Blair, Jr., for Vice-President.
July 9	Submitted to the Senate for its consent a treaty between the United States and the Emperor of China (Burlingame Treaty).
July 18	Suggested to the Congress that it consider a Constitutional Amendment abolishing the Electoral College

and permitting direct election of the President by the people.

October 10 — Issued an order to the Army that it must not interfere in any general or local election.

December 8 — In his last message to Congress again asked for the repeal of the offensive Reconstruction Acts.

December 25 — Extended executive pardon to all former Confederates without exception.

1869

February 22 — Vetoed a protective tariff measure on imported copper and copper ore.
Death of son Robert.

RETIREMENT AND RETURN TO POLITICS

March 4 — Grant sworn into office as Eighteenth President. Johnson did not attend the ceremony.

March 12 — Attended a banquet in his honor in Baltimore.

March 17 — Said "farewell" to former Secretary of the Navy Gideon Welles, his strongest Cabinet backer.

March 18 — Left Washington to return home to Greeneville after an absence of eight years.

October — Suffered narrow defeat in an attempt to win a Senate seat from Tennessee.

1872

Fall — Failed to win election as Congressman-at-large from Tennessee.

1873

Summer — Suffered an attack of Asiatic cholera that took much of his strength. He never completely recovered.

October   Visited Washington to ask, "What kind of government
                       have we now?"

1875

January 26   Elected United States Senator from Tennessee.

March 4   Took his seat in the Senate of the 44th Congress.

March 22   Made his last speech in the Senate, an attack on the
                       Grant administration.

July 29   Suffered a stroke in the home of daughter Mary John-
                       son Stover near Elizabethtown, Tennessee.

July 31   Died at age 66.

August 3   Buried in Greeneville in what later became Andrew
                       Johnson National Cemetery.

1876

January 15   Eliza McCardle Johnson died.

DOCUMENTS

DOCUMENTS

FIRST STATEMENT AS PRESIDENT
April 15, 1865

Johnson was as stunned as the rest of the nation at the news of the murder of Lincoln. This was his first official statement as President. He asked the Lincoln Cabinet to continue to serve and suggested that his actions of the past would serve as clues to his intentions for the future.

GENTLEMEN: I must be permitted to say that I have been almost overwhelmed by the announcement of the sad event which has so recently occurred. I feel incompetent to perform duties so important and responsible as those which have been so unexpectedly thrown upon me. As to an indication of any policy which may be pursued by me in the administration of the Government, I have to say that that must be left for development as the Administration progresses. The message or declaration must be made by the acts as they transpire. The only assurance that I can now give of the future is reference to the past. The course which I have taken in the past in connection with this rebellion must be regarded as a guaranty of the future. My past public life, which has been long and laborious, has been founded, as I in good conscience believe, upon a great principle of right, which lies at the basis of all things. The best energies of my life have been spent in endeavoring to establish and perpetuate the principles of free government, and I believe that the Government in passing through its present perils will settle down upon priciples consonant with popular rights more permanent and enduring than heretofore. I must be permitted to say, if I understand the feelings of my own heart, that I have long labored to ameliorate and elevate the condition of the great mass of the American people. Toil and an honest advocacy of the great principles of free government have been my lot. Duties have been mine; consequences are God's. This has been the foundation of my political creed, and I feel that in the end the Government will triumph and that these great principles will be permanently established.

In conclusion, gentlemen, let me say that I want your encouragement and countenance. I shall ask and rely upon you and others in carring the Government through its present perils. I feel in making this request that it will be heartily responded to by you and all other patriots and lovers of the rights and interests of a free people.

31

A PROCLAMATION OF MOURNING
April 25, 1865

*Again Johnson's executive order reflected the state of
mind of the nation. The reference to the Acting Secretary
of State was a grim reminder that Secretary Seward had
been seriously wounded by a would-be assassin and thus
would be incapacitated for some time to come.*

Whereas, by my direction, the Acting Secretary of State, in a notice
to the public of the 17th, requested the various religious denomina-
tions to assemble on the 19th instant, on the occasion of the obsequies
of Abraham Lincoln, late President of the United States, and to observe
the same with appropriate ceremonies; but

Whereas our country has become one great house of mourning,
where the head of the family has been taken away, and believing that
a special period should be assigned for again humbling ourselves
before Almighty God, in order that the bereavement may be sanctified
to the nation:

Now, therefore, in order to mitigate that grief on earth which can
only be assugaed by communion with the Father in heaven, and in compliance with the wishes of Senators and Representatives in Congress,
communicated to me by resolutions adopted at the National Capitol, I,
Andrew Johnson, President of the United States, do hereby appoint
Thursday, the 25th day of May next, to be observed, wherever in the
United States the flag of the country may be respected, as a day of
humiliation and mourning, and I recommend my fellow-citizens then
to assemble in their respective places of worship, there to unite in
solemn service to Almight God in memory of the good man who has
been removed, so that all shall be occupied at the same time in con-
templation of his vitures and in sorrow for his sudden and violent
end. . . .

                            ANDREW JOHNSON

PROCLAMATION OF REWARD
May 2, 1865

*Johnson jumped to the conclusion (as did many others)
that the leaders of the Confederacy had conspired in the
murder of Lincoln. Clay, Thompson, and Sanders were
unofficial peace "commissioners" to whom Lincoln had
granted a safe conduct to Washington. Cleary was Clay's
clerk, and Tucker was in canada with the "commissioners." The assumption was that the three visitors to Washington had arranged with Booth et al. for the assassination on the orders of Jefferson Davis.*

Whereas it appears from evidence in the Bureau of Military Justice
that the atrocious murder of the late President, Abraham Lincoln,
and the attempted assassination of the Hon. William H. Seward, Secretary of State, were incited, concerted, and procured by and between
Jefferson Davis, late of Richmond, Va., and Jacob Thompson, Clement
C. Clay, Beverley Tucker, George N. Sanders, William C. Cleary,
and other rebels and traitors against the Government of the United
States harbored in Canada:

Now, therefore, to the end that justice may be done, I, Andrew
Johnson, President of the United States, do offer and promise for the
arrest of said persons, or either of them, within the limits of the
United States, so that they can be brought to trial, the following rewards:

One hundred thousand dollars for the arrest of Jefferson Davis.

Twenty-five thousand dollars for the arrest of Clement C. Clay.

Twenty-five thousand dollars for the arrest of Jacob Thompson,
late of Mississippi.

Twenty-five thousand dollars for the arrest of George N. Sanders.

Twenty-five thousand dollars for the arrest of Beverley Tucker.

Ten thousand dollars for the arrest of William C. Cleary, late
clerk of Clement C. Clay.

The Provost-Marshal-General of the United States is directed to
cause a description of said persons, with notice of the above rewards,
to be published. . . .

ANDREW JOHNSON

THE END OF THE BLOCKADE
May 22, 1865

The last of the armies of the Confederacy east of the Mississippi River (General Richard Taylor's) had surrendered on May 4, 1865, and Johnson decided to terminate the blockade that had played such an important role in the victory. Military prudence dictated holding the blockade on the Texas ports until Confederate General Kirby Smith surrendered the forces west of the Mississippi on May 26.

Whereas by the proclamation of the President of the 11th day of April last certain ports of the United States therein specified, which had previously been subject to blockade, were, for objects of public safety, declared, in conformity with previous special legislation of Congress, to be closed against foreign commerce during the national will, to be thereafter expressed and made known by the President; and

Whereas events and circumstances have since occurred which, in my judgment, render it expedient to remove that restriction, except as to the ports of Galveston, La Salle, Brazos de Santiago (Point Isabel), and Brownsville, in the State of Texas:

Now, therefore, be it known that I, Andrew Johnson, President of the United States, do hereby declare that the ports aforesaid, not excepted as above, shall be open to foreign commerce from and after the 1st day of July next; that commercial intercourse with the said ports may from that time be carried on, subject to the laws of the United States and in pursuance of such regulations as may be prescribed by the Secretary of the Treasury. . . .

                                             ANDREW JOHNSON

PROCLAMATION OF AMNESTY AND PARDON
May 29, 1865

As did Lincoln, Johnson proposed to offer a blanket pardon to former Confederates willing to take an oath of loyalty. Not all were eligible as there were exceptions. Johnson added only one exception to Lincoln's list — the thirteenth below. However like any President, Johnson could grant executive clemency to any individual not eligible for the blanket pardon. Johnson proceeded to do this at a rate that first shocked and then enraged the Republican Radicals.

Whereas the President of the United States, on the 8th day of December A.D. 1863, and on the 26th day of March, A.D. 1864, did, with the object to suppress the existing rebellion, to induce all persons to return to their loyalty, and to restore the authority of the United States, issue proclamations offering amnesty and pardon to certain persons who had, indirectly or by implication, participated in the said rebellion; and

Whereas many persons who had so engaged in said rebellion have, since the issuance of said proclamations, failed or neglected to take the benefits offered thereby; and

Whereas many persons who have been justly deprived of all claim to amnesty and pardon thereunder by reason of their participation, directly or by implication, in said rebellion and continued hostility to the Government of the United States may be restored and that peace, order, and freedom may be established, I, Andrew Johnson, President of the United States, do proclaim and declare that I hereby grant to all persons who have, directly or indirectly, participated in the existing rebellion, except as hereinafter excepted, amnesty and pardon, with restoration of all rights of property, except as to slaves and except in cases where legal proceedings under the laws of the United States providing for the confiscation of property of persons engaged in rebellion have been instituted; but upon the condition, nevertheless, that every such person shall take and subscribe the following oath (or affirmation) and thenceforeward keep and maintain said oath inviolate, and which oath shall be registered for permanent preservation and shall be of the tenor and effect following, to wit:

I,   , do solemnly swear (or affirm), in presence of Almighty God, that I will henceforth faithfully support, protect, and defend the Constitution of the United States and the Union of the States thereunder, and that I will in like manner abide by and faithfully support all laws and proclamations which have been made during the existing rebellion with reference to the emancipation of slaves. So help me God.

The following classes of persons are excepted from the benefits of this proclamation:

First. All who are or shall have been pretended civil or diplomatic officers or otherwise domestic or foreign agents of the pretended Confederate government.

Second. All who left judicial stations under the United States to aid the rebellion.

Third. All who shall have been military or naval officers of said pretended Confederate government above the rank of colonel in the army or lieutenant in the navy.

Fourth. All who left seats in the Congress of the United States to aid the rebellion.

Fifth. All who resigned or tendered resignations of their commissions in the Army or Navy of the United States to evade duty in resisting the rebellion.

Sixth. All who have engaged in any way in treating otherwise than lawfully as prisoners of war persons found in the United States service as officers, soldiers, seamen, or in other capacities.

Seventh. All persons who have been or are absentees from the United States for the purpose of aiding the rebellion.

Eighth. All military and naval officers in the rebel service who were educated by the Government in the Military Academy at West Point or the United States Naval Academy.

Ninth. All persons who held the pretended offices of governors of States in insurrection against the United States.

Tenth. All persons who left their homes within the jurisdiction and protection of the United States and passed beyond the Federal military lines into the pretended Confederate States for the purpose of aiding the rebellion.

Eleventh. All persons who have been engaged in the destruction of the commerce of the United States upon the high seas and all persons who have made raids into the United States from Canada or been engaged in destroying the commerce of the United States upon the lakes and rivers that separate the British Provinces from the United States.

Twlfth. All persons who, at the time when they seek to obtain the benefits hereof by taking the oath herein prescribed, are in military, naval, or civil confinement or custody, or under bonds of the civil, military, or naval authorities or agents of the United States as prisoners of war, or persons detained for offenses of any kind, either before or after conviction.

Thirteenth. All persons who have voluntarily participated in said rebellion and the estimated value of whose taxable property is over $20,000.

Fourteenth. All persons who have taken the oath of amnesty as prescribed in the President's proclamation of December 8, A.D. 1863, or an oath of allegiance to the Government of the United States since the date of said proclamation and who have not thenceforward kept and maintained the same inviolate.

Provided, That special application may be made to the President for pardon by any person belonging to the excepted classes, and such clemency will be liberally extended as may be consistent with the facts of the case and the peace and dignity of the United States.

The Secretary of State will establish rules and regulations for administering and recording the said amnesty oath, so as to insure its benefit to the people and guard the Government against fraud. . . .

ANDREW JOHNSON

THE PLAN FOR RESTORATION
May 29, 1865

*With Congress not in session Johnson set out to bring the
former Confederate States back into the Union under his
own plan for Reconstruction. William W. Holden was named
Provisional Governor of North Carolina with orders to
supervise the reorganization of the state. Within two
months Johnson issued similar orders for six other southern
states. Johnson believed that the remaining ex-Confeder-
ate states including Tennessee were far enough along in
the process not to require provisional governors.*

Whereas the fourth section of the fourth article of the Constitution
of the United States declares that the United States shall guarantee to
every State in the Union a republican form of government and shall protect each of them against invasion and domestic violence; and

Whereas the President of the United States is by the Constitution
made Commander in Chief of the Army and Navy, as well as chief
civil executive officer of the United States, and is bound by solemn
oath faithfully to executed; and

Whereas the rebellion which has been waged by a portion of the
people of the United States against the properly constituted authorities
of the Government thereof in the most violent and revolting form, but
whose organized and armed forces have now been almost entirely overcome, has in its revolutionary progress deprived the people of the
State of North Carolina of all civil government; and

Whereas it becomes necessary and proper to carry out and enforce
the obligations of the United States to the people of North Carolina in
securing them in the enjoyment of a republican form of government:

Now, therefore, in obedience to the high and solemn duties imposed
upon me by the Constitution of the United States and for the purpose of
enabling the loyal people of said State to organize a State government
whereby justice may be established, domestic tranquility insured, and
loyal citizens protected in all their rights of life, liberty, and property,
I, Andrew Johnson, President of the United States and Commander in
Chief of the Army and Navy of the United States, do hereby appoint
William W. Holden provisional governor of the State of North Carolina,
whose duty it shall be, at the earliest practicable period, to prescribe
such rules and regulations as may be necessary and proper for con-
vening a convention composed of delegates to be chosen by that portion
of the people of said State who are loyal to the United States, and no
others, for the purpose of altering or amending the constitution thereof,
and with authority to exercise within the limits of said State all the
powers necessary and proper to enable such loyal people of the State
of North Carolina to restore said State to its constitutional relations
to the Federal Government and to present such a republican form of

State government as will entitle the State to the guaranty of the United States therefor and its people to protection by the United States against invasion, insurrection, and domestic violence: Provided, That in any election that may be hereafter held for choosing delegates to any State convention as aforesaid no person shall be qualified as an elector or shall be eligible as a member of such convention unless he shall have previously taken and subscribed the oath of amnesty as set forth in the President's proclamation of May 29, A.D. 1865, and is a voter qualified as prescribed by the constitution and laws of the State of North Carolina in force immediately before the 20th day of May, A.D. 1861, the date of the so-called ordinance of secession; and the said convention, when convened, or the legislature that may be thereafter assembled, will prescribe the qualification of electors and the eligibility of persons to hold office under the constitution and laws of the State — a power the people of the several States composing the Federal Union have rightfully exercised from the origin of the Government to the present time. . . .

ANDREW JOHNSON

EXECUTIVE ORDER FOR VENGEANCE
June 2, 1865

In this order Johnson decided that the Lincoln assassins would be tried by military tribunal rather than in the regular Washington criminal courts. Thus the prisoners were tried under conditions bordering on the barbaric, their heads enclosed in heavy cloth bags, etc. While few doubted the guilt of the three men executed, the execution of Mary Surratt was a cruel miscarriage of justice.

EXECUTIVE CHAMBER,
Washington City, May 1, 1865.

Whereas the Attorney-General of the United States hath given his opinion that the persons implicated in the murder of the late President, Abraham Lincoln, and the attempted assassination of the Hon. William H. Seward, Secretary of State, and in an alleged conspiracy to assassinate other officers of the Federal Government at Washington City, and their aiders and abettors, are subject to the jurisdiction of and lawfully triable before a military commission –

It is ordered:

First. That the assistant adjutant-general detail nine competent military officers to serve as a commission for the trial of said parties and that the Judge-Advocate-General proceed to prefer charges against said parties for their alleged offenses and bring them to trial before said military commission; that said trial or trials be conducted by the said Judge-Advocate-General, and as recorder thereof, in person, aided by such assistant or special judge-advocate as he may designate, and that said trials be conducted with all diligence consistent with the ends of justice; the said commission to sit without regard to hours. . . .

ANDREW JOHNSON

EXECUTIVE ORDER FOR THE FREEDMEN'S BUREAU
June 2, 1865

Johnson acted to end the confusion created when Treasury Department officials attempted to gain control of abandoned southern land on the grounds of tax delinquency. Some Radical Republicans had hoped to settle freed men on these lands and on lands confiscated from ex-Confederates. Johnson dashed these hopes through his pardon policy.

EXECUTIVE MANSION,
Washington, D.C. June 2, 1865

Whereas by an act of Congress approved March 3, 1865, there was established in the War Department a Bureau of Refugees, Freedmen, and Abandoned Lands, and to which, in accordance with the said act of Congress, is committed the supervision and management of all abandoned lands and the control of all subjects relating to refugees and freedmen from rebel States, or from any district of country within the territory embraced in the operations of the Army, under such rules and regulations as may be prescribed by the head of the Bureau and approved by the President; and

Whereas it appears that the management of abandoned lands and subjects relating refugees and freedmen, as aforesaid, have been and still are, by orders based on military exigencies or legislation based on previous statutes, partly in the hands of military officers disconnected with said Bureau and Partly in charge of officers of the Treasury Department: It is therefore

Ordered, That all officers of the Treasury Department, all military officers, and all others in the service of the United States turn over to the authorized officers of said Bureau all abandoned lands and property contemplated in said act of Congress approved March 3, 1865, establishing the Bureau of Refugees, Freedmen, and Abandoned Lands, that may now be under or within their control. They will also turn over to such officers all funds collected by tax or otherwise for the benefit of refugees or freedmen or accruing from abandoned lands or property set apart for their use, and will transfer to them all official records connected with the administration of affairs which pertain to said Bureau.

ANDREW JOHNSON

FIRST ANNUAL MESSAGE TO CONGRESS
December 4, 1865

Johnson had thirty-three weeks in which to deal with Reconstruction without Congress. By the time that Congress agreed to receive this message it had already refused to seat southern Congressmen elected under Johnson's plan and had taken the first steps towards assuming control. In this message Johnson refused to accept the "state suicide" thesis and warned that as President he had no authority to order southern states to grant the vote to Freedmen. By implication Congress lacked the same authority.

WASHINGTON, December 4, 1865

Fellow-Citizens of the Senate and House of Representatives:

To express gratitude to God in the name of the people for the preservation of the United States is my first duty in addressing you. Our thoughts next revert to the death of the late President by an act of parricidal treason. The grief of the nation is still fresh. It finds some solace in the consideration that he lived to enjoy the highest proof of its confidence by entering on the renewed term of the Chief Magistracy to which he had been elected; that he brought the civil war substantially to a close; that his loss was deplored in all parts of the Union, and that foreign nations have rendered justice to his memory. His removal cast upon me a heavier weight of cares than ever devolved upon any one of his predecessors. To fulfill my trust I need the support and confidence of all who are associated with me in the various departments of Government and the support and confidence of the people. There is but one way in which I can hope to gain their necessary aid. It is to state with frankness the principles which guide my conduct, and their application to the present state of affairs, well aware that the efficiency of my labors will in a great measure depend on your and their undivided approbation. . . .

I found the States suffering from the effects of a civil war. Resistance to the General Government appeared to have exhausted itself. The United States had recovered possession of their forts and arsenals, and their armies were in the occupation of every State which had attempted to secede. Whether the territory within the limits of those States should be held as conquered territory, under military authority emanating from the President as the head of the Army, was the first question that presented itself for decision.

Now military governments, established for an indefinite period, would have offered no security for the early suppression of discontent, would have divided the people into the vanquishers and the vanquished, and would have envenomed hatred rather than have restored affection. Once established, no precise limit to their continuance was conceivable. They would have occasioned an incalculable and exhausting expense. Peaceful emigration to and from that portion of the country is one of the best means that can be thought of for the restoration of harmony, and that emigration would have been prevented; for what emigrant from abroad, what industrious citizen at home, would place himself willingly under military rule? The chief persons who would have followed in the train of the Army would have been dependents on the General Government or men who expected profit from the miseries of their erring fellow-citizens. The powers of patronage and rule which would have been exercised under the President, over a vast and populous and naturally wealthy region are greater than, unless under extreme necessity, I should be willing to intrust to any one man. They are such as, for myself, I could never, unless on occasions of great emergency, consent to exercise. The willful use of such powers, if continued through a period of years, would have endangered the purity of the general administration and the liberties of the States which remained loyal.

Besides, the policy of military rule over a conquered territory would have implied that the States whose inhabitants may have taken part in the rebellion had by the act of those inhabitants ceased to exist. But the true theory is that all pretended acts of secession were from the beginning null and void. The States can not commit treason nor screen the individual citizens who may have committed treason any more than they can make valid treaties or engage in lawful commerce with any foreign power. The States attempting to secede placed themselves in a condition where their vitality was impaired, but not extinguished; their functions suspended, but not destroyed.

But if any State neglects or refuses to perform its offices there is the more need that the General Government should maintain all its authority and as soon as practicable resume the exercise of all its functions. On this principle I have acted, and have gradually and quietly, and by almost imperceptible steps, sought to restore the rightful energy of the General Government and of the States. To that end provisional governors have been appointed for the States, conventions called, governors elected, legislatures assembled, and Senators and Representatives chosen to the Congress of the United States. . . .

I know very well that this policy is attended with some risk; that for its success it requires at least the acquiescence of the States which it concerns; that it implies an invitation to those States, by renewing their allegiance to the United States, to resume their functions as States of the Union. But it is a risk that must be taken. In the choice of difficulties it is the smallest risk; and to diminish and if possible to remove all danger, I have felt it incumbent on me to assert one other power of the General Government – the power of pardon. As no State can throw a defense over the crime of treason, the power of pardon is exclusively vested in the executive government of the United States. In exercising that power I have taken every precaution to connect it with the clearest recognition of the binding force of the laws of the United States and an unqualified acknowledgment of the great social change of condition in regard to slavery which has grown out of the war. . . .

The relations of the General Government toward the 4,000,000 inhabitants whom the war has called into freedom have engaged my most serious consideration. On the propriety of attempting to make the freedmen electors by the proclamation of the Executive I took for my counsel the Constitution itself, the interpretations of that instrument by its authors and their contemporaries, and recent legislation by Congress. When, at the first movement toward independence, the Congress of the United States instructed the several States to institute governments of their own, they left each State to decide for itself the conditions for the enjoyment of the elective franchise. During the period of the Confederacy there continued to exist a very great diversity in the qualifications of electors in the several States, and even within a State a distinction of qualifications prevailed with regard to the officers who were to be chosen. The Constitution of the United States recognizes these diversities when it enjoins that in the choice of members of the House of Representatives of the United States "the electors in each State shall have the qualifications requisite for electors of the most numerous branch of the State legislature." After the formation of the Constitution it remained, as before, the uniform usage for each State to enlarge the body of its electors according to its own judgment, and under this system one State after another has proceeded to increase the number of its electors, until now universal suffrage, or something very near it, is the general rule. So fixed was this reservation of power in the habits of the people and so unquestioned has been the interpretation of the Constitution that during the civil war the late President never harbored the purpose — certainly never avowed the purpose — of disregarding it; and in the acts of Congress during that period nothing can be found which, during the continuance of hostilities, much less after their close, would have sanctioned any departure by the Executive from a policy which has so uniformly obtained. Moreover, a concession of the elective franchise to the freedmen by act of the President of the United States must have been extended to all colored men, wherever found, and so must have established a change of suffrage in the Northern, Middle, and Western States, not less than in the Southern and Southwestern. Such an act would have created a new class of voters, and would have been an assumption of power by the President which nothing in the Constitution or laws of the United States would have warranted. . . .

But while I have no doubt that now, after the close of the war, it is not competent for the General Government to extend the elective franchise in the several States, it is equally clear that good faith requires the security of the freedmen in their liberty and their property, their right to labor, and their right to claim the just return of their labor. I can not too strongly urge a dispassionate treatment of this subject, which should be carefully kept aloof from all party strife. We must equally avoid hasty assumptions of any natural impossibility for the two races to live side by side in a state of mutual benefit and good will. The experiment involves us in no inconsistency; let us, then, go on and make that experiment in good faith, and not be too easily disheartened. The country is in need of labor, and the freedmen are in need of employment, culture, and protection. While their right of voluntary migration and expatriation is not to be questioned, I would not advise their forced removal and colonization. Let us rather encourage them to honorable and useful industry, where it may be beneficial to themselves and to the country; and, instead of hasty anticipations of the certainty of failure, let there by nothing wanting to the fair trial of the experiment. . . .

ANDREW JOHNSON

VETO OF EXTENSION OF FREEDMEN'S BUREAU
February 19, 1866

Under the original law the Bureau would have gone out of existence one year after the end of the war. Congress authorized an indefinite extension, and Johnson's veto astounded his friends and foes alike. Johnson was incorrect in stating that the purpose of the Bureau was to help end slavery. In view of the oppressive measures already passed by southern legislatures against the freedmen, Johnson's view of the southern courts was incredibly naive. Nevertheless the Senate sustained the veto, and the matter rested for the time being.

WASHINGTON, February 19, 1866

To the Senate of the United States:

I have examined with care the bill, which originated in the Senate and has been passed by the two Houses of Congress, to amend an act entitled "An act to establish a bureau for the relief of freedmen and refugees," and for other purposes. Having with much regret come to the conclusion that it would not be consistent with the public welfare to give my approval to the measure, I return the bill to the Senate with my objections to its becoming a law. . . .

In time of war it was eminently proper that we should provide for those who were passing suddenly from a condition of bondage to a state of freedom. But this bill proposes to make the Freedmen's Bureau, established by the act of 1865 as one of many great and extraordinary military measures to suppress a formidable rebellion, a permanent branch of the public administration, with its powers greatly enlarged. I have no reason to suppose, and I do not understand it to be alleged, that the act of March, 1865, has proved deficient for the purpose for which it was passed, although at that time and for a considerable period thereafter the Government of the United remained unacknowledged in most of the States whose inhabitants had been involved in the rebellion. The institution of slavery, for the military destruction of which the Freedmen's Bureau was called into existence as an auxiliary, has been already effectually and finally abrogated throughout the whole country by an amendment of the Constitution of the United States, and practically its eradication has received the assent and concurrence of most of those States in which it at any time had an existence. I am not, therefore, able to discern in the condition of the country anything to justify an apprehension that the powers and agencies of the Freedmen's Bureau, which were effective for the protection of freedmen and refugees during the actual continuance of hostilities and of African servitude, will now, in a time of peace and after the abolition of slavery, prove inadequate to the same proper ends. If I am correct in these views, there can be no necessity for the enlargement of the powers of the Bureau, for which provision is made in the bill. . . .

There is still further objection to the bill, on grounds seriously affecting the class of persons to whom it is designed to bring relief. It will tend to keep the mind of the freedman in a state of uncertain expectation and restlessness, while to those among whom he lives it will be a source of constant and vague apprehension.

Undoubtedly the freedman should be protected, but he should be protected by the civil authorities, especially by the exercise of all the constitutional powers of the courts of the United States and of the States. . . .

I can not but add another very grave objection to this bill. The Constitution imperatively declares, in connection with taxation, that each State shall have at least one Representative, and fixes the rule for the number to which, in future times, each State shall be entitled. It also provides that the Senate of the United States shall be composed of two Senators from each State, and adds with peculiar force "that no State, without its consent, shall be deprived of its equal suffrage in the Senate." The original act was necessarily passed in the absence of the States chiefly to be affected, because their people were then contumaciously engaged in the rebellion. Now the case is changed, and some, at least, of those States are attending Congress by loyal representatives, soliciting the allowance of the constitutional right for representation. At the time, however, of the consideration and the passing of this bill there was no Senator or Representative in Congress from the eleven States which are to be mainly affected by its provisions. The very fact that reports were and are made against the good disposition of the people of that portion of the country is an additional reason why they need and should have representatives of their own in Congress to explain their condition, reply to accusations, and assist by their local knowledge in the perfecting of measures immediately affecting themselves. . . .

ANDREW JOHNSON

VETO OF CIVIL, RIGHTS ACT
March 27, 1866

The Civil Rights Act which included the first definition of citizenship was passed by a coalition of moderates and Radicals, and Johnson's veto served to drive the moderates closer to the camp of the Radicals. On April 9, the act was repassed over the veto by a nearly unanimous Republican vote. It was the first major piece of legislation in the Nation's history to go into law over a veto. Then Congress passed a new Freedmen's Bureau Act and repassed that over a veto.

WASHINGTON, D.C., March 27, 1866

To the Senate of the United

I regret that the bill, which has passed both House of Congress, entitled "An act to protect all persons in the United States in their civil rights and furnish the means of their vindication," contains provisions which I can not approve consistently with my sense of duty to the whole people and my obligations to the Constitution of the United States. I am therefore constrained to return it to the Senate, the House in which it originated, with my objections to its becoming a law.

The right of Federal citizenship thus to be conferred on the several excepted races before mentioned is now for the first time proposed to be given by law. If, as is claimed by many, all persons who are native born already are, by virtue of the Constitution, citizens of the United States, the passage of the pending bill can not be necessary to make them such. If, on the other hand, such persons are not citizens, as may be assumed from the proposed legislation to make them such, the grave question presents itself whether, when eleven of the thirty-six States are unrepresented in Congress at the present time, it is sound policy to make our entire colored population and all other excepted classes citizens of the United States. . . .

In the next place, this provision of the bill seems to be unnecessary, as adequate judicial remedies could be adopted to secure the desired end without invading the immunities of legislators, always important to be preserved in the interest of public liberty; without assailing the independence of the judiciary, always essential to the preservation of individual rights; and without impairing the efficiency of ministerial officers, always necessary for the maintenance of public peace and order. The remedy proposed by this section seems to be in this respect not only anomalous, but unconstitutional; for the Constitution guarantees nothing with certainty if it does not insure to the several States the right of making and executing laws in regard to all matters arising within their jurisdiction, subject only to the restriction that in cases of conflict with the Constitution and constitutional laws of the United States the latter should be held to be the supreme law of the land. . . .

I do not propose to consider the policy of this bill. To me the details of the bill seem fraught with evil. The white race and the black race of the South have hitherto lived together under the relation of master and slave — capital owning labor. Now, suddenly, that relation is changed, and as to ownership capital and labor are divorced. They stand now each master of itself. In this new relation, one being necessary to the other, there will be a new adjustment, which both are deeply interested in making harmonious. Each has equal power in settling the terms, and if left to the laws that regulate capital and labor it is confidently believed that they will satisfactorily work out the problem. Capital, it is true, has more intelligence, but labor is never so ignorant as not to understand its own interests, not to know its own value, and not to see that capital must pay that value. . . .

ANDREW JOHNSON

VETO OF FIRST RECONSTRUCTION ACT
March 2, 1867

Under this act the existing reconstruction governments in the south would be destroyed, and the south placed under military rule. On the same day of the veto Congress re-passed the Act, the vote in the House being 135 to 48; and in the Senate, 38 to 10. In like manner Congress en-acted into law the Tenure of Office Act which appeared to limit Johnson's control over his Cabinet. It also re-duced Johnson's authority over the army.

WASHINGTON, March 2, 1867

To the House of Representatives:

I have examined the bill "to provide for the more efficient govern-ment of the rebel States" with the care and anxiety which its transcen-dent importance is calculated to awaken. I am unable to give it my as-sent, for reasons so grave that I hope a statement of them may have some influence on the minds of the patriotic and enlightened men with whom the decision must ultimately rest.

I submit to Congress whether this measure is not in its whole character, scope, and object without precedent and without authority, in palpable conflict with the plainest provisions of the Constitution, and utterly destructive to those great principles of liberty and human-ity for which our ancestors on both sides of the Atlantic have shed so much blood and expended so much treasure.

The ten States named in the bill are divided into five districts. For each district an officer of the Army, not below the rank of a brig-adier-general, is to be appointed to rule over the people; and he is to be supported with an efficient military force to enable him to perform his duties and enforce his authority. Those duties and that authority, as defined by the third section of the bill, are "to protect all persons in their rights of person and property, to suppress insurrection, dis-order, and violence, and to punish or cause to be punished all dis-turbers of the public peace or criminals." The power thus given to the commanding officer over all the people of each district is that of an absolute monarch. His mere will is to take the place of all law. . . .

It is plain that the authority here given to the military officer a-mounts to absolute despotism. But to make it still more unendurable, the bill provides that it may be delegated to as many subordinates as he chooses to appoint, for it declares that he shall "punish or cause to be punished." Such a power has not been wielded by any monarch in England for more than five hundred years. In all that time no people who speak the English language have borne such servitude. It reduces the whole population of the ten States — all persons, of every color, sex, and condition, and every stranger within their limits – to the most abject and degrading slavery. No master ever had a control so absolute over the slaves as this bill gives to the military officers over both white and colored persons. . . .

I come now to a question which is, if possible, still more important. Have we the power to establish and carry into execution a measure like this? I answer, Certainly not, if we derive our authority from the Constitution and if we are bound by the limitations which it imposes. . . .

This is a bill passed by Congress in time of peace. There is not in any one of the States brought under its operation either war or insurrection. The laws of the States and of the Federal Government are all in undisturbed and harmonious operation. The courts, State and Federal, are open and in the full exercise of their proper authority. Over every State comprised in these five military districts, life, liberty, and property are secured by State laws and Federal laws, and the National Constitution is everywhere in force and everywhere obeyed. . . .

The United States are bound to guarantee to each State a republican form of government. Can it be pretended that this obligation is not palpably broken if we carry out a measure like this, which wipes away every vestige of republican government in ten States and puts the life, property, liberty, and honor of all the people in each of them under the domination of a single person clothed with unlimited authority? . . .

The bill also denies the legality of the governments of ten of the States which participated in the ratification of the amendment to the Federal Constitution abolishing slavery forever within the jurisdiction of the United States and practically excludes them from the Union. If this assumption of the bill be correct, their concurrence can not be considered as having been legally given, and the important fact is made to appear that the consent of three-fourths of the States – the requisite number – has not been constitutionally obtained to the ratification of that amendment, thus leaving the question of slavery where it stood before the amendment was officially declared to have become a part of the Constitution. . . .

ANDREW JOHNSON

THIRD ANNUAL MESSAGE TO CONGRESS
December 3, 1867

*In spite of Johnson's defeat in the Congressional elec-
tions of 1866, the President indicated that he was still
convinced of the justice of his course and of the error of
Congress. Actually there was no chance that this Congress would repeal the First Reconstruction Act. The new
Congress, called into session months ahead of schedule
by the lame duck Congress to whom Johnson sent this
message, would be even more Radical. Johnson remained
either bravely determined or foolishly stubborn depending
upon one's view point.*

WASHINGTON, December 3, 1867

Fellow-Citizens of the Senate and House of Representatives:

The continued disorganization of the Union, to which the President
has so often called the attention of Congress, is yet a subject of pro-
found and patriotic concern. We may, however, find some relief from
that anxiety in the reflection that the painful political situation, although before untried by ourselves, is not new in the experience of
nations. Political science, perhaps as highly perfected in our own time
and country as in any other, has not yet disclosed any means by which
civil wars can be absolutely prevented. An enlightened nation, however,
with a wise and beneficent constitution of free government, may diminish their frequency and mitigate their severity by directing all its
proceedings in accordance with its fundamental law. . . .

On this momentous question and some of the measures growing out
of it I have had the misfortune to differ from Congress, and have expressed my convictions without reserve, though with becoming defer-
ence to the opinion of the legislative department. Those convictions
are not only unchanged, but strengthened by subsequent events and
further reflection. The transcendent importance of the subject will be a
sufficient excuse for calling your attention to some of the reasons
which have so strongly influenced my own judgment. The hope that we
may all finally concur in a mode of settlement consistent at once with
our true interests and with our sworn duties to the Constitution is too
natural and too just to be easily relinquished. . . .

This is so plain that it has been acknowledged by all branches of
the Federal Government. The Executive (my predecessor as well as
myself) and the heads of all the Departments have uniformly acted upon the principle that the Union is not only undissolved, but indissoluble.
Congress submitted an amendment to the Constitution to be ratified by
the Southern States, and accepted their acts of ratification as a necessary and lawful exercise of their highest function. If they were not
States, or were States out of the Union, their consent to a change in
the fundamental law of the Union would have been nugatory, and Con-

gress in asking it committed a political absurdity. The judiciary has also given the solemn sanction of its authority to the same view of the case. The judges of the Supreme Court have included the Southern States in their circuits, and they are constantly, in banc and elsewhere, exercising jurisdiction which does not belong to them unless those States are States of the Union. . . .

Being sincerely convinced that these views are correct, I would be unfaithful to my duty if I did not recommend the repeal of the acts of Congress which place ten of the Southern States under the domination of military masters. If calm reflection shall satisfy a majority of your honorable bodies that the acts referred to are not only a violation of the national faith, but in direct conflict with the Constitution, I dare not permit myself to doubt that you will immediately strike them from the statute book. . . .

The acts of Congress in question are not only objectionable for their assumption of ungranted power, but many of their provisions are in conflict with the direct prohibitions of the Constitution. The Constitution commands that a republican form of government shall be guaranteed to all the States; that no person shall be deprived of life, liberty, or property without due process of law, arrested without a judicial warrant, or punished without a fair trial before an impartial jury; that the privilege of habeas corpus shall not be denied in time of peace, and that no bill of attainder shall be passed even against a single individual. Yet the system of measures established by these acts of Congress does totally subvert and destroy the form as well as the substance of republican government in the ten States to which they apply. It binds them hand and foot in absolute slavery, and subjects them to a strange and hostile power, more unlimited and more likely to be abused than any other now known among civilized men. It tramples down all those rights in which the essence of liberty consists, and which a free government is always most careful to protect. It denies the habeas corpus and the trial by jury. Personal freedom, property, and life, if assailed by the passion, the prejudice, or the rapacity of the ruler, have no security whatever. It has the effect of a bill of attainder or bill of pains and penalties, not upon a few individuals, but upon whole masses, including the millions who inhabit the subject States, and even their unborn children. These wrongs, being expressly forbidden, can not be constitutionally inflicted upon any portion of our people, no matter how they may have come within our jurisdiction, and no matter whether they live in States, Territories, or districts. . . .

ANDREW JOHNSON

VETO OF ELECTORAL COLLEGE ACT
July 20, 1868

Although Johnson had just escaped conviction in the Senate by only one vote, this message indicated his conviction of the constitutionality of his position. Once again he pointed out the basic inconsistency of his opponents. Two days prior to this veto he had urged the Congress to pass a Constitutional amendment abolishing the Electoral College. As usual this act was passed over the veto, and the electoral votes of Mississippi, Texas, and Virginia were not counted in the Grant-Seymour election of 1868.

WASHINGTON, D.C., July 20, 1868

To the Senate of the United States:

I have given to the joint resolution entitled "A resolution excluding from the electoral college the votes of States lately in rebellion which shall not have been reorganized" as careful examination as I have been able to bestow upon the subject during the few days that have intervened since the measure was submitted for my approval.

Feeling constrained to withhold my consent, I herewith return the resolution to the Senate, in which House it originated, with a brief statement of the reasons which have induced my action. This joint resolution is based upon the assumption that some of the States whose inhabitants were lately in rebellion are not now entitled to representation in Congress and participation in the election of President and Vice-President of the United States.

Having heretofore had occasion to give in detail my reasons for dissenting from this view, it is not necessary at this time to repeat them. It is sufficient to state that I continue strong in my conviction that the acts of secession, by which a number of the States sought to dissolve their connection with the other States and to subvert the Union, being unauthorized by the Constitution and in direct violation thereof, were from the beginning absolutely null and void. It follows necessarily that when the rebellion terminated the several States which had attempted to secede continued to be States in the Union, and all that was required to enable them to resume their relations to the Union was that they should adopt the measures necessary to their practical restoration as States. Such measures were adopted, and the legitimate result was that those States, having conformed to all the requirements of the Constitution, resumed their former relations, and became entitled to the exercise of all the rights guaranteed to them by its provisions.

The joint resolution under consideration, however, seems to assume that by the insurrectionary acts of their respective inhabitants those

States forfeited their rights as such, and can never again exercise them except upon readmission into the Union on the terms prescribed by Congress. If this position be correct, it follows that they were taken out of the Union by virtue of their acts of secession, and hence that the war waged upon them was illegal and unconstitutional. We would thus be placed in this inconsistent attitude, that while the war was commenced and carried on upon the distinct ground that the Southern States, being component parts of the Union, were in rebellion against the lawful authority of the United States, upon its termination we resort to a policy of reconstruction which assumes that it was not in fact a rebellion, but that the war was waged for the conquest of territories assumed to be outside of the constitutional Union.

The mode and manner of receiving and counting the electoral votes for President and Vice-President of the United States are in plain and simple terms prescribed by the Constitution. That instrument impera- tively requires that "the President of the Senate shall, in the presence of the Senate and House of Representatives, open all the certificates, and the votes shall then be counted." Congress has, therefore, no power, under the Constitution, to receive the electoral votes or reject them. The whole power is exhausted when, in the presence of the two Houses, the votes are counted and the result declared. In this respect the power and duty of the President of the Senate are, under the Con- stitution, purely ministerial. When, therefore, the joint resolution de- clares that no electoral votes shall be received or counted from States that since the 4th of March, 1867, have not "adopted a constitu- tion of State government under which a State government shall have organized," a power is assumed which is nowhere delegated to Con- gress, unless upon the assumption that the State governments organ- ized prior to the 4th of March, 1867, were illegal and void.

The joint resolution, by implication at least, concedes that these States were States by virtue of their organization prior to the 4th of March, 1867, but denies to them the right to vote in the election of President and Vice-President of the United States. It follows either that this assumption of power is wholly unauthorized by the Constitu- tion or that the States so excluded from voting were out of the Union by reason of the rebellion, and have never been legitimately restored. Being fully satisfied that they were never out of the Union, and that their relations thereto have been legally and constitutionally restored, I am forced to the conclusion that the joint resolution, which deprives them of the right to have their votes for President and Vice-President received and counted, is in conflict with the Constitution, and that Congress has no more power to reject their votes than those of the States which have been uniformly loyal to the Federal Union.

It is worthy of remark that if the States whose inhabitants were re- cently in rebellion were legally and constitutionally organized and restored to their rights prior to the 4th of March, 1867, as I am satis- fied they were, the only legitimate authority under which the election for President and Vice-President can be held therein must be derived from the governments instituted before that period. It clearly follows that all the State governments organized in those States under act of Congress for that purpose, and under military control, are illegitimate and of no validity whatever; and in that view the votes cast in those States for President and Vice-President, in pursuance of acts passed since the 4th of March, 1867, and in obedience to the so-called reconstruction acts of Congress, can not be legally received and counted, will be those cast in pursuance of the laws in force in the several States prior to the legislation by Congress upon the subject of reconstruction. . . .

If Congress were to provide by law that the votes of none of the States should be received and counted if cast for a candidate who differed in political sentiment with a majority of the two Houses, such legislation would at once be condemned by the country as an unconstitutional and revolutionary usurpation of power. It would, however, be exceedingly difficult to find in the Constitution any more authority for the passage of the joint resolution under consideration than for an enactment looking directly to the rejection of all votes not in accordance with the political preferences of a majority of Congress. No power exists in the Constitution authorizing the joint resolution or the supposed law — the only difference being that one would be more palpably unconstitutional and revolutionary than the other. Both would rest upon the radical error that Congress has the power to prescribe terms and conditions to the right of the people of the States to cast their votes for President and Vice-President.

For the reasons thus indicated I am constrained to return the joint resolution to the Senate for such further action thereon as Congress may deem necessary.

ANDREW JOHNSON

FOURTH ANNUAL MESSAGE TO CONGRESS
December 9, 1868

Now a lame duck, President Johnson for the last time called for the repeal of the measures that he considered to be oppressive and the cause for the failure of Reconstruction. Of his four specific proposals of a positive nature, two have long been enacted and a third is at this time (1970) under consideration.

WASHINGTON, December 9, 1868

Fellow-Citizens of the Senate and House of Representatives:

Upon the reassembling of Congress it again becomes my duty to call your attention to the state of the Union and to its continued disorganized condition under the various laws which have been passed upon the subject of reconstruction.

It may be safely assumed as an axiom in the government of states that the greatest wrongs inflicted upon a people are caused by unjust and arbitrary legislation, or by the unrelenting decrees of despotic rulers, and that the timely revocation of injurious and oppressive measures is the greatest good that can be conferred upon a nation. The legislator or ruler who has the wisdom and magnanimity to retrace his steps when convinced or error will sooner or later be rewarded with the respect and gratitude of an intelligent and patriotic people.

Our own history, although embracing a period less than a century, affords abundant proof that most, if not all, of our domestic troubles are directly traceable to violations of the organic law and excessive legislation. The most striking illustrations of this fact are furnished by the enactments of the past three years upon the question of reconstruction. After a fair trial they have substantially failed and proved pernicious in their results, and there seems to be no good reason why they should longer remain upon the statute book. States to which the Constitution guarantees a republican form of government have been reduced to military dependencies, in each of which the people have been made subject to the arbitrary will of the commanding general. Although the Constitution requires that each State shall be represented in Congress, Virginia, Mississippi, and Texas are yet excluded from the two Houses, and, contrary to the express provisions of that instrument, were denied participation in the recent election for a President and Vice-President of the United States. The attempt to place the white population under the domination of persons of color in the South has impaired, if not destroyed, the kindly relations that had previously existed between them; and mutual distrust has engendered a feeling of animosity which, leading in some instances to collision and bloodshed, has prevented that cooperation between the two races so essential to the success of industrial enterprise in the Southern States. Nor have the inhabitants of those States alone suffered from the disturbed condition of affairs growing out of these Congressional enactments. The entire Union has been agitated by grave apprehensions of troubles which might again involve the peace of the nation; its interests have been injuriously affected by the derangement of business and labor, and the consequent want of prosperity throughout that portion of the country.

The Federal Constitution — the magna charta of American rights, under whose wise and salutary provisions we have successfully conducted all our domestic and foreign affairs, sustained ourselves in peace and in war, and become a great nation among the powers of the earth — must assuredly be now adequate to the settlement of questions growing out of the civil war, waged alone for its vindication. This great fact is made most manifest by the condition of the country when Congress assembled in the month of December, 1865. Civil strife had ceased, the spirit of rebellion had spent its entire force, in the Southern States the people had warmed into national life, and throughout the whole country a healthy reaction in public sentiment had taken place. By the application of the simple yet effective provisions of the Constitution the executive department, with the voluntary aid of the States, had brought the work of restoration as near completion as was within the scope of its authority, and the nation was encouraged by the prospect of an early and satisfactory adjustment of all its difficulties. Congress, however, intervened, and, refusing to perfect the work so nearly consummated, declined to admit members from the unrepresented States, adopted a series of measures which arrested the progress of restoration, frustrated all that had been so successfully accomplished, and, after three years of agitation and strife, has left the country further from the attainment of union and fraternal feeling than at the inception of the Congressional plan of reconstruction. It needs no argument to show that legislation which has produced such baneful consequences should be abrogated, or else made to conform to the genuine principles of republican government.

Under the influence of party passion and sectional prejudice, other acts have been passed not warranted by the Constitution. Congress has already been made familiar with my views respecting the "tenure-of-office bill." Experience has proved that its repeal is demanded by the best interests of the country, and that while it remains in force the President can not enjoin that rigid accountability of public officers so essential to an honest and efficient execution of the laws. It revocation would enable the executive department to exercise the power of appointment and removal in accordance with the original design of the Federal Constitution.

The act of March 2, 1867, making appropriations for the support of the Army for the year ending June 30, 1868, and for other purposes,

contains provisions which interfere with the President's constitutional functions as Commander in Chief of the Army and deny to States of
the Union the right to protect themselves by means of their own milita.
These provisions should be at once annulled; for while the first might,
in times of great emergency, seriously embarrass the Executive in
efforts to employ and direct the common strength of the nation for its
protection and preservation, the other is contrary to the express declaration of the Constitution that "a well-regulated militia being necessary to the security of a free state, the right of the people to keep and
bear arms shall not be infringed."

It is believed that the repeal of all such laws would be accepted
by the American people as at least a partial return to the fundamental
principles of the Government, and an indication that hereafter the Constitution is to be made the nation's safe and unerring guide. They can
be productive of no permanent benefit to the country, and should not
be permitted to stand as so many monuments of the deficient wisdom
which has characterized our recent legislation. . . .

In my message to Congress December 4, 1865, it was suggested
that a policy should be devised which, without being oppressive to the
people, would at once begin to effect a reduction of the debt, and, if
persisted in, discharge it fully within a definite number of years.
The Secretary of the Treasury forcibly recommends legislation of this
character, and justly urges that the longer it is deferred the more difficult must become its accomplishment. We should follow the wise pre-
cedents established in 1789 and 1816, and without further delay make
provision for the payment of our obligations at as early a period as
may be practicable. The fruits of their labors should be enjoyed by
our citizens rather than used to build up and sustain moneyed monopolies in our own and other lands. Our foreign debt is already computed by the Secretary of the Treasury at $850,000,000; citizens of
foreign countries receive interest upon a large portion of our secur-
ities, and American taxpayers are made to contribute large sums
for their support. The idea that such a debt is to become permanent
should be at all times discarded as involving taxation too heavy to be
borne, and payment once in every sixteen years, at the present rate
of interest, of an amount equal to the original sum. This vast debt, if
permitted to become permanent and increasing, must eventually be
gathered into the hands of a few, and enable them to exert a dangerous
and controlling power in the affairs of the Government. The borrowers
would become servants to the lenders, the lenders the masters of the
people. We now pride ourselves upon having given freedom to 4,000,000
of the colored race; it will then be our shame that 40,000,000 of people,
by their own toleration of usurpation and profligacy, have suffered
themselves to become enslaved, and merely exchanged slave owners
for a new taskmasters in the shape of bondholders and taxgatherers.
Besides, permanent debts pertain to monarchical governments, and,
tending to monopolies, perpetuities, and class legislation, are totally

irreconcilable with free institutions. Introduced into our republican system, they would gradually but surely sap its foundations, eventually subvert our governmental fabric, and erect upon its ruins a moneyed aristocracy. It is our sacred duty to transmit unimpaired to our posterity the blessings of liberty which were bequeathed to us by the founders of the Republic, and by our example teach those who are to follow us carefully to avoid the dangers which threaten a free and independent people. . . .

The report of the Secretary of War contains information of interest and importance respecting the several bureaus of the War Department and the operations of the Army. The strength of our military force on the 30th of September last was 48,000 men, and it is computed that by the 1st of January next this number will be decreased to 43,000. It is the opinion of the Secretary of War that within the next year a considerable diminution of the infantry force may be made without detriment to the interests of the country; and in view of the great expense attending the military peace establishment and the absolute necessity of retrenchment whereever it can be applied, it is hoped that Congress will sanction the reduction which his report recommends. While in 1860 sixteen thousand three hundred men cost the nation $16,472,000 the sum of $65,682,000 is estimated as necessary for the support of the Army during the fiscal year ending June 30, 1870. The estimates of the War Department for the last two fiscal years were, for 1867, $33,814,461, and for 1868 $25,205,669. The actual expenditures during the same periods were, respectively $95,224,415 and $123,246,648. The estimate submitted in December last for the fiscal year ending June 30, 1869, was $77,124,707; the expenditures for the first quarter, ending the 30th of September last, were $7,219,117 and the Secretary of the Treasury gives $66,000,000 as the amount which will probably be required during the remaining three quarters, if there should be no reduction of the Army – making its aggregate cost for the year considerably in excess of ninety-three millions. The difference between the estimates and expenditures for the three fiscal years which have been named is thus shown to be $175,545,343 for this single branch of the public service. . . .

The acquisition of Alaska was made with the view of extending national jurisdiction and republican principles in the American hemisphere. Believing that a further step could be taken in the same direction, I last year entered into a treaty with the King of Denmark for the purchase of the islands of St. Thomas and St. John, on the best terms then attainable, and with the express consent of the people of those islands. This treaty still remains under consideration in the Senate. A new convention has been entered into with Denmark, enlarging the time fixed for final ratification of the original treaty.

Comprehensive national policy would seem to sanction the acquisition and incorporation into our Federal Union of the several adjacent continental and insular communities as speedily as it can be done peacefully, lawfully, and without any violation of national justice, faith, or honor. Foreign possession or control of those communities has hitherto hindered the growth and impaired the influence of the United States. Chronic revolution and anarchy there would be equally injurious. Each one of them, when firmly established as an independent republic, or when incorporated into the United States, would be a new source of strength and power. Conforming my Administration to these principles, I have on no occasion lent support or toleration to unlawful expeditions set on foot upon the plea of republican propagandism or of national extension or aggrandizement. The necessity, however, of repressing such unlawful movements clearly indicates the duty which rests upon us of adapting our legislative action to the new circumstances of a decline of European monarchical power and influence and the increase of American republican ideas, interests, and sympathies.

It can not be long before it will become necessary for this Government to lend some effective aid to the solution of the political and social problems which are continually kept before the world by the two Republics of the island of St. Domingo, and which are now disclosing themselves more distinctly than heretofore in the island of Cuba. The subject is commended to your consideration with all the more earnestness because I am satisfied that the time has arrived when even so direct a proceeding as a proposition for an annexation of the two Republics of the island of St. Domingo would not only receive the consent of the people interested, but would also give satisfaction to all other foreign nations. . . .

I renew the recommendation contained in my communication to Congress dated the 18th July last — a copy of which accompanies this message — that the judgment of the people should be taken on the propriety of so amending the Federal Constitution that it shall provide—

First.   For an election of President and Vice-President by a direct vote of the people, instaed of through the agency of electors, and making them ineligible for reelection to a second term.

Second.   For a distinct designation of the person who shall discharge the duties of President in the event of a vacancy in that office by the death, resignation, or removal of both the President and Vice-President.

Third.   For the election of Senators of the United States directly by the people of the several States, instead of by the legislatures; and

Fourth.   For the limitation to a period of years of the terms of Federal judges.

Profoundly impressed with the propriety of making these important modifications in the Constitution, I respectfully submit them for the early and mature consideration of Congress. We should, as far as possible, remove all pretext for violations of the organic law, by remedying such imperfections as time and experience may develop, ever remembering that "the constitution which at any time exists until changed by an explicit and authentic act of the whole people is sacredly obligatory upon all."

In the performance of a duty imposed upon me by the Constitution, I have thus communicated to Congress information of the state of the Union and recommended for their consideration such measures as have seemed to me necessary and expedient. If carried into effect, they will hasten the accomplishment of the great and beneficent purposes for which the Constitution was ordained, and which it comprehensively states were "to form a more perfect Union, establish justice, insure domestic tranquillity, provide for the common defense, promote the general welfare, and secure the blessings of liberty to ourselves and our posterity." In Congress are vested all legislative powers, and upon them devolves the responsibility as well for framing unwise and excessive laws as for neglecting to devise and adopt measures absolutely demanded by the wants of the country. Let us earnestly hope that before the expiration of our respective terms of service, now rapidly drawing to a close, an all-wise Providence will so guide our counsels as to strengthen and preserve the Federal Union, inspire reverence for the Constitution, restore prosperity and happiness to our whole people, and promote "on earth peace, good will toward men."

PROCLAMATION OF EXECUTIVE PARDON
December 25, 1868

Johnson granted executive pardon to ex-Confederates without exception.

Whereas the President of the United States has heretofore set forth several proclamations offering amnesty and pardon to persons who had been or were concerned in the late rebellion against the lawful authority of the Government of the United States, which proclamations were severally issued on the 8th day of May, 1865, on the 7th day of September, 1867, and on the 4th day of July, in the present year; and

Whereas the authority of the Federal Government having been reestablished in all the States and Territories within the jurisdiction of the United States, it is believed that such prudential reservations and exceptions as at the dates of said several proclamations were deemed necessary and proper may now be wisely and justly relinquished, and that an universal amnesty and pardon for participation in said rebellion extended to all who have borne any part therein will tend to secure permanent peace, order, and prosperity throughout the land, and to renew and fully restore confidence and fraternal feeling among the whole people, and their respect for and attachment to the National Government, designed by its patriotic founders for the general good.

Now, therefore, be it known that I, Andrew Johnson, President of the United States, by virtue of the power and authority in me vested by the Constitution and in the name of the sovereign people of the United States, do hereby proclaim and declare, unconditionally and without reservation, to all and to every person who, directly or indirectly, participated in the late insurrection or rebellion a full pardon and amnesty for the offense of treason against the United States or of adhering to their enemies during the late civil war, with restoration of all rights, privileges, and immunities under the Constitution and the laws which have been made in pursuance thereof.

ANDREW JOHNSON

VETO OF TARIFF ACT
February 22, 1869

*With only ten days left in the White House Johnson, using
the rhetoric of Andrew Jackson, took a stand against
what he thought was class legislation. It was of little
avail, and it revealed the depth of the division between
the President and the politicians who had once supported
him for vice president. In the next two decades Congres-
ses and Presidents. added more of these measures until a
major segment of the country cried out for relief.*

WASHINGTON, D.C. February 22, 1869

To the House of Representatives:

The accompanying bill, entitled "An act regulating the duties on
important copper and copper ores," is, for the following reasons,
returned, without my approval, to the House of Representatives, in
which branch of Congress it originated.

Its immediate effect will be to diminish the public receipts, for
the object of the bill can not be accomplished without seriously affecting the importation of copper and copper ores, from which a considerable revenue is at present derived. While thus impairing the
resources of the Government, it imposes an additional tax upon an
already overburdened people, who should not be further improveris-
ed that monopolies may be fostered and corporations enriched.

It is represented – and the declaration seems to be sustained by
evidence – that the duties for which this bill provides are nearly or
quite sufficient to prohibit the importation of certain foreign ores of
copper. Its enactment, therefore, will prove detrimental to the ship-
ping interests of the nation, and at the same time destroy the business,
for many years successfully established, of smelting home ores in
connection with a smaller amount of the imported articles. This business, it is credibly asserted, has heretofore yielded the larger share
of the copper production of the country, and thus the industry which
this legislation is designed to encourage is actually less than that which
will be destroyed by the passage of this bill.

It seems also to be evident that the effect of this measure will be
to enhance by 70 per cent the cost of blue vitriol – an article exten-
sively used in dyeing and in the manufacture of printed and colored
cloths. To produce such an augmentation in the price of this commodity will be to discriminate against other great branches of domestic
industry, and by increasing their cost to expose them most unfairly
to the effects of foreign competition. Legislation can neither be wise
nor just which seeks the welfare of a single interest at the expense and
to the injury of many and varied interests at least equally important
and equally deserving the consideration of Congress. Indeed, it is difficult to find any reason which will justify the interference of Govern-

ment with any legitimate industry, except so far as may be rendered necessary by the requirements of the revenue. As has already been stated, however, the legislative intervention proposed in the present instance will diminish, not increase, the public receipts.

The enactment of such a law is urged as necessary for the relief of certain mining interests upon Lake Superior, which, it is alleged, are in a greatly depressed condition, and can only be sustained by an enhancement of the price of copper. If this result should follow the passage of the bill, a tax for the exclusive benefit of a single class would be imposed upon the consumers of copper throughout the entire country, not warranted by any need of the Government, and the avails of which would not in any degree find their way into the Treasury of the nation. If the miners of Lake Superior are in a condition of want, it can not be justly affirmed that the Government should extend charity to them in preference to those of its citizens who in other portions of the country suffer in like manner from destitution. Least of all should the endeavor to aid them be based upon a method so uncertain and in-direct as that contemplated by the bill, and which, moreover, proposes to continue the exercise of its benefaction through an indefinite period of years. It is, besides, reasonable to hope that positive suffering from want, if it really exists, will prove but temporary in a region where agricultural labor is so much in demand and so well compensated. A careful examination of the subject appears to show that the present low price of copper, which alone has induced any depression the min-ing interests of Lake Superior may have recently experienced, is due to causes which it is wholly impolitic, if not impracticable, to contravene by legislation. These causes are, in the main, an increase in the general supply of copper, owing to the discovery and working of remarkably productive mines and to a coincident restriction in the consumption and use of copper by the substitution of other and cheaper metals for industrial purposes. It is now sought to resist by artificial means the action of natural laws; to place the people of the United States, in respect to the enjoyment and use of an essential commodity, upon a different basis from other nations, and especially to compen-sate certain private and sectional interests for the changes and losses which are always incident to industrial progress.

Although providing for an increase of duties, the proposed law does not even come within the range of protection, in the fair acceptation of the term. It does not look to the fostering of a young and feeble inter-est with a view to the ultimate attainment of strength and the capacity of self-support. It appears to assume that the present inability for suc-cessful production is inherent and permanent, and is more likely to increase than to be gradually overcome; yet in spite of this it proposes, by the exercise of the lawmaking power, to sustain that interest and to impose it in hopeless perpetuity as a tax upon the competent and bene-ficent industries of the country.

The true method for the mining interests of Lake Superior to obtain relief, if relief is needed, is to endeavor to make their great natural resources fully available by reducing the cost of production. Special or class legislation can not remedy the evils which this bill is designed to meet. They can only be overcome by laws which will effect a wise, honest, and economical administration of the Government, a reestablishment of the specie standard of value, and an early adjustment of our system of State, municipal, and national taxation (especially the latter) upon the fundamental principle that all taxes, whether collected under the internal revenue or under a tariff, shall interfere as little as possible with the productive energies of the people.

The bill is therefore returned, in the belief that the true interests of the Government and of the people require that it should not become a law.

ANDREW JOHNSON

FIRST NINE ARTICLES OF IMPEACHMENT
March 2, 1868

*Having voted on February 24, 1868, to impeach Johnson,
the House then adopted the articles on which to try him
before the Senate. Although the articles were "stupidly
tautological" they pointed to things that Johnson had in
fact done. There would be little difficulty in proving
this. But did these acts constitute "high crimes and mis-
demeaners?"*

IN THE HOUSE OF REPRESENTATIVES, UNITED STATES,
March 2, 1868

ARTICLES EXHIBITED BY THE HOUSE OF REPRESENTATIVES OF
THE UNITED STATES, IN THE NAME OF THEMSELVES AND ALL
THE PEOPLE OF THE UNITED STATES, AGAINST ANDREW
JOHNSON, PRESIDENT OF THE UNITED STATES, IN MAINTEN-
ANCE AND SUPPORT OF THEIR IMPEACHMENT AGAINST HIM
FOR HIGH CRIMES AND MISDEMEANORS IN OFFICE.

ARTICLE I. That said Andrew Johnson, President of the United
States, on the 21st day of February, A.D. 1868, at Washington, in the
District of Columbia, unmindful of the high duties of his office, of
his oath of office, and of the requirement of the Constitution that he
should take care that the laws be faithfully executed, did unlawfully
and in violation of the Constitution and laws of the United States issue
an order in writing for the removal of Edwin M. Stanton from the office of Secretary for the Department of War, said Edwin M. Stanton
having been theretofore duly appointed and commissioned, by and with
the advice and consent of the Senate of the United States, as such
Secretary; and said Andrew Johnson, President of the United States,
on the 12th day of August, A.D. 1867, and during the recess of said
Senate, having suspended by his order Edwin M. Stanton from said
office, and within twenty days after the first day of the next meeting of
said Senate – that is to say, on the 12th day of December, in the year
last aforesaid – having reported to said Senate such suspension, with
the evidence and reasons for his action in the case and the name of
the person designated to perform the duties of such office temporarily
until the next meeting of the Senate; and said Senate thereafterwards,
on the 13th day of January, A.D. 1868, having duly considered the evidence and reasons reported by said Andrew Johnson for said suspension, and having refused to concur in said suspension, whereby and by
force of the provisions of an act entitled "An act regulating the tenure
of certain civil offices," passed March 2, 1867, said Edwin M. Stanton
did forthwith resume the functions of his office, whereof the said Andrew Johnson had then and there due notice; and said Edwin M. Stanton,
by reason of the premises, on said 21st day of February, being lawfully

entitled to hold said office of Secretary for the Department of War; which said order for the removal of said Edwin M. Stanton is in substance as follows; that is to say:

EXECUTIVE MANSION,
Washington, D.C., February 21, 1868.

HON. EDWIN M. STANTON,
Washington, D.C.

SIR: By virtue of the power and authority vested in me as President by the Constitution and laws of the United States, you are hereby removed from office as Secretary for the Department of War, and your functions as such will terminate upon the receipt of this communication.

You will transfer to Brevet Major-General Lorenzo Thomas, Adjutant-General of the Army, who has this day been authorized and empowered to act as Secretary of War ad interim, all records, books, papers, and other public property now in your custody and charge.

Respectfully, yours,

ANDREW JOHNSON.

which order was unlawfully issued with intent then and there to violate the act entitled "An act regulating the tenure of certain civil offices," passed March 2, 1867, and with the further intent, contrary to the provisions of said act, in violation thereof, and contrary to the provisions of the Constitution of the United States, and without the advice and consent of the Senate of the United States, the said Senate then and there being in session, to remove said Edwin M. Stanton from the office of Secretary for the Department of War, the said Edwin M. Stanton being then and there Secretary for the Department of War, and being then and there in the due and lawful execution and discharge of the duties of said office; whereby said Andrew Johnson, President of the United States, did then and there commit and was guilty of a high misdemeanor in office.

ART. II. That on said 21st day of February, A.D. 1868, at Washington, in the District of Columbia, said Andrew Johnson, President of the United States, unmindful of the high duties of his office, of his oath of office, and in violation of the Constitution of the United States, and contrary to the provisions of an act entitled "An act regulating the tenure of certain civil offices," passed March 2, 1867, without the advice and consent of the Senate of the United States, said Senate then and there being in session, and without authority of law, did, with intent to violate the Constitution of the United States and the act aforesaid, issue and deliver to one Lorenzo Thomas a letter of authority in substance as follows; that is to say:

EXECUTIVE MANSION,
Washington, D.C., February 21, 1868

Brevet Major-General LORENZO THOMAS,
   Adjutant-General United States Army, Washington, D.C.

SIR: The Hon. Edwin M. Stanton having been this day removed from office as Secretary for the Department of War, you are hereby authorized and empowered to act as Secretary of War ad interim, and will immediately enter upon the discharge of the duties pertaining to that office.

Mr. Stanton has been instructed to transfer to you all the records, books, papers, and other public property now in his custody and charge.

Respectfully, yours,

ANDREW JOHNSON

then and there being no vacancy in said office of Secretary for the Department of War; whereby said Andrew Johnson, President of the United States, did then and there commit and was guilty of a high misdemeanor in office.

ART. III.   That said Andrew Johnson, President of the United States, on the 21st day of February, A.D. 1868, at Washington, in the District of Columbia, did commit and was guilty of a high misdemeanor in office in this, that without authority of law, while the Senate of the United States was then and there in session, he did appoint one Lorenzo Thomas to be Secretary for the Department of War ad interim, without the advice and consent of the Senate, and with intent to violate the Constitution of the United States, no vacancy having happened in said office of Secretary for the Department of War during the recess of the Senate, and no vacancy existing in said office at the time, and which said appointment, so made by said Andrew Johnson, of said Lorenzo Thomas, is in substance as follows; that is to say:

EXECUTIVE MANSION,
Washington, D.C., February 21, 1868

Brevet Major-General LORENZO THOMAS,
   Adjutant-General United States Army, Washington, D.C.

SIR: The Hon. Edwin M. Stanton having been this day removed from office as Secretary for the Department of War, you are hereby authorized and empowered to act as Secretary of War ad interim, and will immediately enter upon the discharge of the duties pertaining to that office.

Mr. Stanton has been instructed to transfer to you all the records, books, papers, and other public property now in his custody and charge.

Respectfully, yours,

ANDREW JOHNSON

ART. IV.   That said Andrew Johnson, President of the United States, unmindful of the high duties of his office and his oath of office, in violation of the Constitution and laws of the United States, on the 21st day of February, A.D. 1868, at Washington, in the District of Columbia, did unlawfully conspire with one Lorenzo Thomas, and with other persons to the House of Representatives unknow, with intent, by intimidation and threats, unlawfully to hinder and prevent Edwin M. Stanton, then and there the Secretary for the Department of War, duly appointed under the laws of the United States, from holding said office of Secretary for the Department of War, contrary to and in violation of the Constitution of the United States and of the provisions of an act entitled "An act to define and punish certain conspiracies," approved July 31, 1861; whereby said Andrew Johnson, President of the United States, did then and there commit and was guilty of a high crime in office.

ART. V.   That said Andrew Johnson, President of the United States, unmindful of the high duties of his office and of his oath of office, on the 21st day of February, A.D. 1868, and on divers other days and times in said year before the 2d day of March, A.D. 1868, at Washington, in the District of Columbia, did unlawfully conspire with one Lorenzo Thomas, and with other persons to the House of Representatives unknown, to prevent and hinder the execution of an act entitled "An act regulating the tenure of certain civil offices," passed March 2, 1867, and in pursuance of said conspiracy did unlawfully attempt to prevent Edwin M. Stanton, then and there being Secretary for the Department of War, duly appointed and commissioned under the laws of the United States, from holding said office; whereby the said Andrew Johnson, President of the United States, did then and there commit and was guilty of a high misdemeanor in office.

ART. VI.   That said Andrew Johnson, President of the United States, unmindful of the high duties of his office and of his oath of office, on the 21st day of February, A.D 1868, at Washington, in the District of Columbia, did unlawfully conspire with one Lorenzo Thomas by force to seize, take, and possess the property of the United States in the Department of War, and then and there in the custody and charge of Edwin M. Stanton, Secretary for said Department, contrary to the provisions of an act entitled "An act to define and punish certain conspiracies," approved July 31, 1861, and with intent to violate and disregard an act entitled "An act regulating the tenure of certain civil offices," passed March 2, 1867; whereby said Andrew Johnson, President of the United States, did then and there commit a high crime in office.

ART. VII. That said Andrew Johnson, President of the United States, unmindful of the high duties of his office and of his oath of office, on the 21st day of February, A.D. 1868, at Washington, in the District of Columbia, did unlawfully conspire with one Lorenzo Thomas with intent unlawfully to seize, take, and possess the property of the United States in the Department of War, in the custody and charge of Edwin M. Stanton, Secretary for said Department, with intent to violate and disregard the act entitled "An act regulating the tenure of certain civil offices," passed March 2, 1867; whereby said Andrew Johnson, President of the United States, did then and there commit a high misdemeanor in office.

ART. VIII. That said Andrew Johnson, President of the United States, unmindful of the high duties of his office and of his oath of office, with intent unlawfully to control the disbursement of the moneys appropriated for the military service and for the Department of War, on the 21st day of February, A.D. 1868, at Washington, in the District of Columbia, did unlawfully, and contrary to the provisions of an act entitled "An act regulating the tenure of certain civil offices," passed March 2, 1867, and in violation of the Constitution of the United States, and without the advice and consent of the Senate of the United States, and while the Senate was then and there in session, there being no vacancy in the office of Secretary for the Department of War, and with intent to violate and disregard the act aforesaid, then and there issue and deliver to one Lorenzo Thomas a letter of authority, in writing, in substance as follows; that is to say:

EXECUTIVE MANSION
Washington, D.C., February 21, 1868

Brevet Major-General LORENZO THOMAS,
Adjutant-General United States Army, Washington, D.C.

SIR: The Hon. Edwin M. Stanton having been this day removed from office as Secretary for the Department of War, you are hereby authorized and empowered to act as Secretary of War ad interim, and will immediately enter upon the discharge of the duties pertaining to that office.

Mr. Stanton has been instructed to transfer to you all the records, books, papers, and other public property now in his custody and charge.

Respectfully, yours,

ANDREW JOHNSON

whereby said Andrew Johnson, President of the United States, did then and there commit and was guilty of a high misdemeanor if office.

ART. IX. That said Andrew Johnson, President of the United States, on the 22d day of February, A.D. 1868, at Washington, in the District of Columbia, in disregard of the Constitution and the laws of the United States duly enacted, as Commander in Chief of the Army of the United States, did bring before himself then and there William H. Emory, a major-general by brevet in the Army of the United States, actually in command of the Department of Washington and the military forces thereof, and did then and there, as such Commander in Chief, declare to and instruct said Emory that part of a law of the United States, passed March 2, 1867, entitled "An act making appropriations for the support of the Army for the year ending June 30, 1868, and for other purposes," especially the second section thereof, which provides, among other things, that "all orders and instructions relating to military operations issued by the President or Secretary of War shall be issued through the General of the Army, and in case of his inability through the next in rank," was unconstitutional and in contravention of the commission of said Emory, and which said provision of law had been theretofore duly and legally promulgated by general order for the government and direction of the Army of the United States, as the said Andrew Johnson then and there well knew, with intent thereby to induce said Emory, in his official capacity as commander of the Department of Washington, to violate the provisions of said act and to take and receive, act upon, and obey such orders as he, the said Andrew Johnson, might make and give, and which should not be issued through the General of the Army of the United States, according to the provisions of said act, and with the further intent thereby to enable him, and said Andrew Johnson, to prevent the execution of the act entitled "An act regulating the tenure of certain civil offices," passed March 2, 1867, and to unlawfully prevent Edwin M. Stanton, then being Secretary for the Department of War, from holding said office and discharging the duties thereof; whereby said Andrew Johnson, President of the United States, did then and there commit and was guilty of a high misdemeanor in office.

And the House of Representatives, by protestation, saving to themselves the liberty of exhibiting at any time hereafter any further articles or other accusation or impeachment against the said Andrew Johnson, President of the United States, and also of replying to his answers which he shall make unto the articles herein preferred against him, and of offering proof to the same, and every part thereof, and to all and every other article, accusation, or impeachment which shall be exhibited by them, as the case shall require, do demand that the said Andrew Johnson may be put to answer the high crimes and misdemeanors in office herein charged against him, and that such proceedings, examinations, trials, and judgments may be thereupon had and given as may be agreeable to law and justice.

SCHUYLER COLFAX,
Speaker of the House of Representatives.

EDWARD McPHERSON,
Clerk of the House of Representatives

Attest:

TENTH AND ELEVENTH ARTICLES OF IMPEACHMENT
March 3, 1868

*The tenth article claimed that Johnson had critized Con-
gress. The House added the eleventh as sort of a catch-
all, designed to win Senate votes that might not be cast
for the first ten. Nowhere was there a charge of corrup-
tion in office.*

in the house of representatives, united states

march 3, 1868

The following additional articles of impeachment were agreed to
viz:

ART. X.   That said Andrew Johnson, President of the United
States, unmindful of the high duties of his office and the dignity and
proprieties thereof, and of the harmony and courtesies which ought to
exist and be maintained between the executive and legislative branches
of the Government of the United States, designing and intending to set
aside the rightful authority and powers of Congress, did attempt to
bring into disgrace, ridicule, hatred, contempt, and reproach the
Congress of the United States and the several branches thereof, to
impair and destroy the regard and respect of all the good people of
the United States for the Congress and legislative power thereof
(which all officers of the Government ought inviolably to preserve and
maintain) and to excite the odium and resentment of all the good
people of the United States against Congress and the laws by it duly
and constitutionally enacted; and, in pursuance of his said design and
intent, openly and publicly, and before divers assemblages of the citizens of the United States, convened in divers parts thereof to meet and
receive said Andrew Johnson as the Chief Magistrate of the United
States, did, on the 18th day of August, A.D. 1866, and on divers other
days and times, as well before as afterwards, make and deliver with
a loud voice certain intemperate, inflammatory, and scandalous har-
angues, and did therein utter loud threats and bitter menaces, as well
against Congress as the laws of the United States, duly enacted thereby, amid the cries, jeers, and laughter of the multitudes then assembled and in hearing, . . .

ART. XI.   That said Andrew Johnson, President of the United
States, unmindful of the high duties of his office and of his oath of office, and in disregard of the Constitution and laws of the United States,
did heretofore, to wit, on the 18th day of August, A.D. 1866, at the
city of Washington, in the District of Columbia, by public speech,
declare and affirm in substance that the Thirty-ninth Congress of the
United States was not a Congress of the United States authorized by
the Constitution to exercise legislative power under the same, but,
on the contrary, was a Congress of only part of the States; thereby

denying and intending to deny that the legislation of said Congress was valid or obligatory upon him, the said Andrew Johnson, except in so far as he saw fit to approve the same, and also thereby denying and intending to deny the power of the said Thirty-ninth Congress to propose amendments to the Constitution of the United States; and in pursuance of said declaration the said Andrew Johnson, President of the United States, afterwards, to wit, on the 21st day of February, A.D. 1868, at the city of Washington, in the District of Columbia, did unlawfully, and in disregard of the requirement of the Constitution that he should take care that the laws be faithfully executed, attempt to prevent the execution of an act entitled "An act regulating the tenure of certain civil offices," passed March 2, 1867, by unlawfully devising and contriving, and attempting to devise and contrive, means by which he should prevent Edwin M. Stanton from forthwith resuming the functions of the office of Secretary for the Department of War, notwithstanding the refusal of the Senate to concur in the suspension theretofore made by said Andrew Johnson of said Edwin M. Stanton from said office of Secretary for the Department of War, and also by further unlawfully devising and contriving, and attempting to devise and contrive, means then and there to prevent the execution of an act entitled "An act making appropriations for the support of the Army for the fiscal year ending June 30, 1868 and for other purposes," approved March 2, 1867, and also to prevent the execution of an act entitled "An act to provide for the more efficient government of the rebel States," passed March 2, 1867, whereby the said Andrew Johnson, President of the United States, did then, to wit, on the 21st day of February, A.D. 1868, at the city of Washington, commit and was guilty of a high misdemeanor in office.

SCHUYLER COLFAX,
Speaker of the House of Representatives

EDWARD McPHERSON,
Clerk of the House of Representatives

Attest:

THE SENATE VOTE ON ARTICLE ELEVEN
May 16, 1868

Immediately upon the announcement of Johnson's acquittal under this article the Senate went into recess for ten days so that the Republicans could attend their national convention (which nominated Grant) and to permit public pressure to be brought against the Senators who had voted "innocent." On May 26, the Senate voted on the Second and Third Articles with results identical to the first vote. The Senate then adjourned without voting on the remaining articles.

SATURDAY, MAY 16, 1868.

THE UNITED STATES vs. ANDREW JOHNSON, PRESIDENT

The Chief Justice stated that, in pursuance of the order of the Senate, he would first proceed to take the judgment of the Senate on the eleventh article. The roll of the Senate was called, with the following result:

The Senators who voted "guilty" are Messrs. Anthony, Cameron, Cattell, Chandler, Cole, Conkling, Conness, Corbett, Cragin, Drake, Edmunds, Ferry, Frelinghuysen, Harlan, Howard, Howe, Morgan, Morrill of Maine, Morrill of Vermont, Morton, Nye, Patterson of New Hampshire, Pomeroy, Ramsey, Sherman, Sprague, Stewart, Summer, Thayer, Tipton, Wade, Williams, Willey, Wilson, and Yates – 35.

The Senators who voted "not guilty" are Messrs. Bayard, Buckalew, Davis, Dixon, Doolittle, Fessenden, Fowler, Grimes, Henderson, Hendricks, Johnson, McCreery, Norton, Patterson of Tennessee, Ross, Saulsbury, Trumbull, Van Winkle, and Vickers – 19.

The Chief Justice announced that upon this article thirty-five Senators had voted "guilty" and nineteen Senators "not guilty," and declared that two-thirds of the Senators present not having pronounced him guilty, Andrew Johnson, President of the United States, stood acquitted of the charges contained in the eleventh article of impeachment.

BIBLIOGRAPHICAL AIDS

BIBLIOGRAPHICAL AIDS

The emphasis in this and other volumes in the Presidential Chronologies series is on the administration of the Presidents. The more important works on the other aspects of their lives, before and after their terms, are included since they may contribute to an understanding of the presidential careers. This is especially true in this volume on Johnson since he worked on two levels of Reconstruction. As Military Governor of Tennessee he started that state on the road to reunion, and then as President he assumed the responsibility for all.

The following bibliography is critically selected. Many of the titles do not concern Johnson directly as northern Radical Republicans assumed roles if increasing importance between 1865 and 1868. Many additional titles can be found in the bibliography of James G. Randall and David Donald, The Civil War and Reconstruction. There is also a usefull bibliography in Lawanda Cox and John H. Cox, Politics, Principle, and Prejudice, 1865–1866. For recent articles in the scholarly journals consult the Reader's Guide to Periodical Literature and Social Sciences and Humanistic Index.

Additional chronological information not included in this volume because it did not relate directly to the President may be found in the Encyclopedia of American History, edited by Richard B. Morris, revised edition (New York, 1965).

Asterisks after titles refer to books currently available in paperback editions.

SOURCE MATERIAL

The Johnson papers are in the Library of Congress and are available on microfilm (fifty-five reels) with a printed index. The Seward papers are located at the University of Rochester. As of this writing the National Archives is making available the records of the Freedmen's Bureau on microfilm. Many of Johnson's letters and reports as Military Governor can be found in War of the Rebellion: Official Records of the Union and Confederate Armies (128 vols., 1880–1901), Series I, Vols. 23–25, 30–32, and 45–52. Other Johnson letters can be found in Roy Basler (ed.), Collected Works of Abraham Lincoln (9 vols., 1953–1955).

JOHNSON BIOGRAPHIES

Unfortunately there is no good Johnson biography available. Two overly sympathetic studies were made in the 1920's, Robert W. Winston, <u>Andrew Johnson: Plebeian and Patriot</u>, New York, 1928, and Lloyd Paul Stryker, <u>Andrew Johnson: A Study in Courage</u>, New York, 1929. Stryker's biography is badly biased in Johnson's favor and even considering the year of publication it displays a venomous racial prejudice. Winston did note that Johnson did not understand the changes that were taking place in the United States and could not abandon, "the simple uncomplicated Democratic doctrines of Jackson. . . ." Lately Thomas (Robert V.P. Steele) <u>The First President Johnson: The Three Lives of the Seventeenth President of the United States of America</u>, New York, 1968, is no better. Written more for amateurs and hero worshipers, Thomas's subtitle points to the major flaw in the book. Johnson had one life and not three, and there was a monotenous sameness about that life. Fortunately there are a number of excellent studies of the critical years of Johnson's life to cover for the lack of a complete biography.

ESSAYS

Albjerg, Marguerite H, "The New York Press and Andrew Johnson," <u>South Atlantic Quarterly</u>, 26 (1927), 404–416.

Cole, Arthur C. "Lincoln and the Presidential Election of 1864," <u>Transactions of the Illinois State Historical Society,</u> (1917), 130-138.

Cox, John H. and Lawanda, "General O. O. Howard and the 'Misrepresented Bureau'," "<u>Journal of Southern History</u>, 19 (November, 1953), 427-456.

Donald, David, "Why They Impeached Andrew Johnson," <u>American Heritage</u>, 8 (1956), 21-25.

Dudley, Harold M. "The Election of 1864," <u>Mississippi Valley Historical Review,</u> 18 (1932), 500-518.

Gipson, Lawrence H. "The Statesmanship of President Johnson: A Study of the Presidential Reconstruction Policy," <u>Mississippi Valley Historical Review,</u> 2 (1915), 363-383.

Gloneck, James F. "Lincoln, Johnson, and the Baltimore Ticket," <u>Abraham Lincoln Quarterly</u>, 6 (1951), 255-271.

Graf, LeRoy P. "Andrew Johnson and the Coming of the War,"
Tennessee Historical Quarterly, 19 (1960), 208-221.

Haws, Willard. "Andrew Johnson's Reputation," East Tennessee
Historical Society Publications, 31 (1959), 1-31.

Holmes, Jack D. L. "The Underlying Causes of the Memphis Race
Riot of 1866," Tennessee Historical Quarterly, 17 (1958), 195-221.

Merrill, Louis T. "General Benjamin F. Butler in Washington,"
Columbia Historical Society Records, 39 (1938).

Nettles, Curtis. "Andrew Johnson and the South," South Atlantic
Quarterly, 25 (1926), 55-64.

Parks, Joseph H. "Memphis Under Military Rule," East Tennessee
Historical Society Publications, 14 (1942), 31-58.

Phifer, Gregg. "Andrew Johnson Takes a Trip," Tennessee Historical Quarterly, 2 (1952), 3-22.

Riddleberger, Patrick W. "The Radicals' Abandonment of the Negro
during Reconstruction," Journal of Negro History, 45 (1960),
88-102.

Scroggs, Jack B. "Southern Reconstruction: A Radical View," Journal
of Southern History, 24 (1958), 407-429.

Sproat, John G. "Blueprint for Radical Reconstruction," Journal of
Southern History 23 (1957), 25-44.

Williams, Harry. "Andrew Johnson as a Member of the Committee
on the Conduct of the War," East Tennessee Historical Society
Publications," '2 (1940), 70-83.

MONOGRAPHS

Abernethy, Thomas P. From Frontier to Plantation in Tennessee.
U. of Alabama Press, 1932.

Beale, Howard K. The Critical Year, A Study of Andrew Johnson and
Reconstruction. New York, 1958. Beale took economic factors
into consideration and stated that Johnson's error lay in his failure to use these factors to drive a wedge between the eastern and
western Radicals.

Bentley, George H. History of the Freedmen's Bureau. Philadelphia, 1955.

Bowers, Claude G. The Tragic Era. Cambridge, 1929.* In the years immediately following publication this work had enormous impact on scholarly opinion regarding the Reconstruction. Although it is outdated by modern research it must be included in any bibliography for its historiographic significance.

Brodie, Fawn M. Thaddeus Stevens: Scourge of the South. New York, 1959.*

Buck, Paul H. The Road to Reunion, 1865-1900. Boston, 1937.*

Clark, Blanche H. The Tennessee Yoeman, 1840-1860. New York, 1942.

Coulter, Merton E. William G. Brownlow: Fighting Parson from the Southern Highlands. New York, 1937.

Cox, Lawanda and John H. Cox. Politics, Principle, and Prejudice, 1865-1866. New York, 1963. The authors wrote that Johnson was attempting to form a new political party based on his own leadership and Reconstruction politices. He failed because he would not or could not make concessions to Republican majority opinion.

Dewitt, David M. The Impeachment and Trial of Andrew Johnson. Madison, Wisconsin, 1967.

Donald, David. The Politics of Reconstruction, 1963-1867. Baton Rouge, 1965.

Dorris, Jonathan T. Pardon and Amnesty under Lincoln and Johnson. Chapel Hill, 1953.

DuBois, W.E.B. Black Reconstruction in America. New York, 1935.*

Dunning, William A. Reconstruction, Political and Economic, 1865-1877. New York, 1907.*

Franklin, John Hope. Reconstruction after the Civil War. Chicago, 1961.*

Hall, Clifton. Andrew Johnson: Military Governor of Tennessee. Princeton, 1916. An excellent study of little known years of Johnson's life.

Henry, Robert S. The Story of Reconstruction. Indianapolis, 1938.

James, Joseph B. The Framing of the Fourteenth Amendment. Urbana, Illinois, 1956.*

Korngold, Ralph. Thaddeus Stevens: A Being Darkly Wise and Rudely Great. New York, 1955.

Kutler, Stanley I. Judicial Power and Reconstruction Politics. Chicago, 1968.

Lomask, Milton. Andrew Johnson: President on Trial. New York, 1960. A very readable account of Johnson's years as President. It included concise accounts of Johnson's principal contemporaries.

McKitrick, Eric. Andrew Johnson and Reconstruction. Chicago, 1960.* This is the best work available describing Johnson the "outsider" struggling to cope with gradually increasing radicalism and Democrats who refused to compromise.

Milton, George F. The Age of Hate: Andrew Johnson and the Radicals. Hamden, Conn., 1930.

Mooney, Chase C. Slavery in Tennessee. Bloomington, 1957.

Moore, Guy E. The Case of Mrs. Surratt. Norman, 1954.

Nevins, Allan. The Emergence of Modern America, 1865-1878. New York, 1927.

Patrick, Rembert W. The Reconstruction of the Nation. Oxford, 1967.* Each chapter concludes with an updated and select bibliography.

Pratt, Fletcher. Stanton: Lincoln's Secretary of War. New York, 1935.

Sharkey, Robert P. Money, Class, and Party: An Economic Study of the Civil War and Reconstruction. Baltimore, 1959.*

Stampp, Kenneth. The Era of Reconstruction, 1865-1877. New York, 1965.*

Temple, Oliver P. East Tennessee and the Civil War. Cincinnati, 1899.

Thomas, Benjamin and Harold Hyman. Stanton: The Life and Times of Lincoln's Secretary of War. New York, 1962.

Trefousse, Hans L. The Radical Republicans: Lincoln's Vanguard for Racial Justice. New York, 1969.

VanDeusen, Glyndon G.   William Henry Seward. New York, 1967.

Wilson, Theodore B. The Black Codes of the South. U. of Ala. Press.
    Here it is pointed out that the Black Codes were little understood
    in the North and that only the most damning fractions were pub-
    lished in northern newspapers.

NAME INDEX